Acknowledgments

Since Mel's best-selling book, *Active Learning*, was published back in 1996, the two of us, both individually and as a team, have shared applications of the many strategies *Active Learning* contains to Jewish subject matter. We've traveled from coast to coast (e.g. San Diego, Seattle, Portland, ME, Springfield, MA) sharing these ideas with Jewish educators. Thousands of you have tried out active Jewish learning techniques and have told us what worked well for you. We appreciate all of you, especially participants at CAJE conferences and meetings of the Educators' Assembly, who have engaged in this experimentation, and have given us the gift of encouragement and constructive feedback. *Active Jewish Learning* is a result of this collaboration.

Shoshana wants to especially thank her colleagues at the Auerbach Central Agency for Jewish Education and to Audrey Friedman-Marcus, former publisher of Alternatives in Religious Education, for their creative ideas and further development of active Jewish learning. Mel owes a deep debt of gratitude to Sivasailam Thiagarajan (better known as Thiagi), Bob Pike, Karen Lawson, and Sharon Bowman who have been a renewing source of active learning advice in the secular world.

Thanks also to Joel Grishaver and the Torah Aura team for their enthusiastic support for this present publication.

Our family is a special source of joy, love, and support. Shmuel, Lisa, and Gabe, our children, son-in-law Daniel and daughter-in-law Sara, have been steadfast boosters of our passion for active Jewish learning. Our precious grandchildren, Noam, Jonah, Yaakov, Adira, Meir, and Chana, make it all worthwhile.

Active Jewish Learning

57 Strategies to Enliven Your Class

Shoshana Silberman, Ed.D.
and Mel Silberman, Ph.D.

Torah Aura Productions

ISBN 10: 1-934527-23-9

ISBN 13: 978-1-934527-23-8

Torah Aura Productions • 4423 Fruitland Avenue, Los Angeles, CA 90058
(800) BE-Torah • (800) 238-6724 • (323) 585-7312 • fax (323) 585-0327
E-MAIL <misrad@torahaura.com> • Visit the Torah Aura website at www.torahaura.com

MANUFACTURED IN THE USA

Contents

Preface

You can tell students what they need to know very *fast*.

But they will forget what you tell them even *faster*.

Yes, there is a whole lot more to teaching than telling! Learning is not an automatic consequence of pouring information into a student's head.

It requires the learner's own mental involvement and doing. Explanation and demonstration by themselves will never lead to real, lasting learning. Only learning that is active will do this.

What makes learning "active"? When learning is active, students do most of the work. They use their brains, studying ideas, solving problems, and applying what they learn. Active learning is fast-paced, fun, supportive, and personally engaging. Often students are out of their seats, moving about and thinking aloud.

Why is it necessary to make learning active? In order to learn something well, it helps to hear it, see it, ask questions about it, and discuss it with others. Above all else, students need to "do it." That includes figuring out things by themselves, coming up with examples, trying out skills, and doing assignments that depend on the knowledge they already have or must acquire.

While we know that students learn best by doing, how do we promote active Jewish learning? This book contains specific, practical strategies that can be used for almost any subject you may teach. They are designed to enliven your classroom. Some are a lot of fun, and some are downright serious, but they all are intended to deepen learning and retention.

Active Jewish Learning brings together in one source a comprehensive collection of instructional strategies. It includes ways to get students active from the start through activities that build teamwork and immediately get them thinking about the subject matter. There are also techniques for conducting full-class learning and small-group learning, stimulating discussion and debate, practicing skills, and even getting the students to teach each other. Finally, there are methods for reviewing what's been learned and assessing what has been accomplished.

You can use *Active Jewish Learning* as an instant grab bag of ways to teach all kinds of subjects, including:

- Hebrew reading and language
- Bible
- Siddur
- Shabbat and holidays
- Jewish ceremonies and practices
- History
- Values and ethics
- Life cycle

Active Jewish Learning is for any Jewish educator, experienced or novice, who teaches in supplementary or day schools, as well as in informal settings. You can use its creative ideas with children as young as six. It's also ideal for children up to the age of bar/bat mitzvah. Students in high school programs will also love its motivating strategies. (No doubt you'll get more than a few great ideas for adult education classes as well.)

Active Jewish Learning begins with "The *Tachlis* (Essentials) of Active Jewish Learning." The chapter contains numerous tips to start you off on organizing and facilitating active learning. Included are ways to form groups, obtain participation, create classroom layouts, facilitate discussion, and more!

The fifty-seven techniques described throughout the remainder of *Active Jewish Learning* are concrete strategies that enable you to apply active learning to your subject matter. These techniques are divided into three sections.

How to Get Students Active From the Start

This section contains icebreakers and other kinds of opening activities for any kind of class. The techniques are designed to do one or more of the following:

- *Getting to Know You*—helping students to become acquainted with one another or creating a spirit of cooperation and interdependence.
- *Immediate Learning Involvement*—creating initial interest in the subject matter.

In addition, these techniques encourage students to take an active role right from the beginning.

How to Teach Information, Skills, and Attitudes Actively

This section contains instructional techniques that can be used when you are at the heart of your lesson. The techniques are designed to avoid or reinforce teacher-led instruction. A wide range of alternatives is provided, all of which gently push students to think, feel, and apply. They include:

- *Full-Class Learning*—teacher-led instruction that stimulates the entire class.
- *Class Discussion*—dialogue about and debate of key issues
- *Cooperative Learning*—assignments done collaboratively in small groups of students.
- *Affective Learning*—activities that help students to examine their feelings, values, and attitudes.
- *Skill Development*—learning and practicing skills.
- *Computer-mediated Learning*—using technology to reinforce what has been taught.

How to Make Learning Unforgettable

This section contains ways to conclude a class so that students reflect on what they have learned and celebrate their accomplishments. The focus is not on what you have told them, but on what they take away. The techniques are designed to do one or more of the following:

- *Review*—recalling and summarizing what has been learned.
- *Self-assessment*—evaluating changes in knowledge, skills, or attitudes.
- Shalom, L'Hitraot—communicating the thoughts, feelings, and concerns students have at the end.

Each of the fifty-seven techniques you are about to learn are described and illustrated in the following ways:

- *Overview*—a statement about the purpose of the technique and the setting in which it is appropriate.
- *Procedure*—step-by-step instructions and illustrations to show you how to use the technique and apply it to your subject matter.

- *Variations*—suggestions for alternative ways to use the technique.
- *Examples*—specific ways to apply the technique to a variety of subjects and with students of different ages.

One final word: Use these techniques as they are or adapt them to fit your needs. And add your own creativity! As you do, bear in mind these suggestions.

- Don't experiment wildly. Try out one new method at a time before going on to another.
- When you introduce a method to students, sell it as an alternative to the usual way of doing things that you think might be worth a try. Obtain their feedback.
- Don't overload students with too many activities. *Less is often more.* Use just a few to enliven your class.
- Make your instructions crystal clear. Demonstrate or illustrate what students are expected to do so that there is no confusion that might distract them from getting the most out of the technique.
- If an activity is not successful on your first try, review what you did and make changes for a better outcome the next time you try it. Also, the more practice you get with an activity, the more you'll be a "pro" at it!

Kol Tuv!

SECTION 1

The Tachlis (Essentials) of Active Jewish Learning

Before reading the active learning strategies described in this book, you may find it useful to consider what we refer to as the *tachlis,* the "essentials", of active Jewish learning. These are quick tips for organizing and facilitating learning activities so that they are as active as possible. We have developed these tips to help you identify, at a glance, several choices available at different points in the course of instruction. Many of the ideas you are about to read are well known. You may already be using several of them. We hope that having an organized list of them, however, will make your job of facilitating active learning easier. Think of these lists as teaching menus from which you might select the option you need at any given moment to make learning active.

Setting Up an Active Classroom

The physical environment in a classroom can make or break active learning. No setup is ideal, but there are many options to choose from. The "interior decorating" of active learning is fun and challenging (especially when the furniture is less than ideal). In some cases, furniture can be easily rearranged to create different setups. Even traditional desks or desk chairs can be grouped together to form tables and other arrangements. If you choose to do so, ask students to help move desks, tables, and chairs. That gets them active, too.

Most of the layouts described below are not meant to be permanent arrangements. As long as your furniture is movable, it should be possible to use a few of these layouts as you see fit. You will also find suggestions on how to utilize even the most traditional classroom environments for active learning.

1. **U Shape:** This is an all-purpose setup. The students have a reading/writing surface, can see you and/or a visual medium easily, and are in face-to-face contact with one another. It's also easy to pair up students. The arrangement is ideal for distributing learning materials quickly to students, since you can enter the U and walk to different points with sets of materials.

   You can set up desks, desk chairs, or tables in a squared-off U:

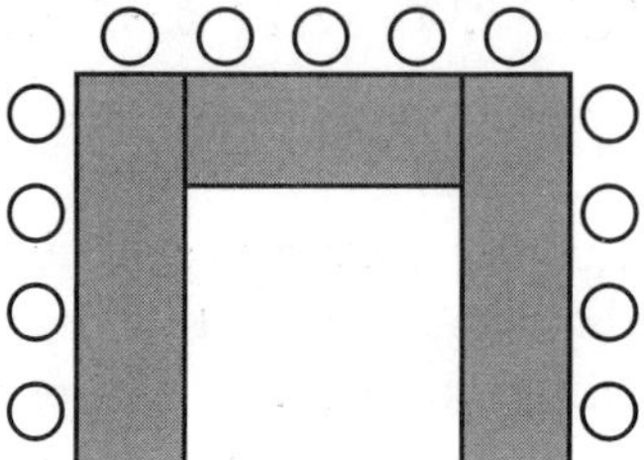

figure 1.1

   Be sure there is enough perimeter space in the room so that subgroups of three or more students can pull back from the desks or tables and face each other.

   You can also arrange chairs, desks, or oblong tables in a U that looks more like a semicircle:

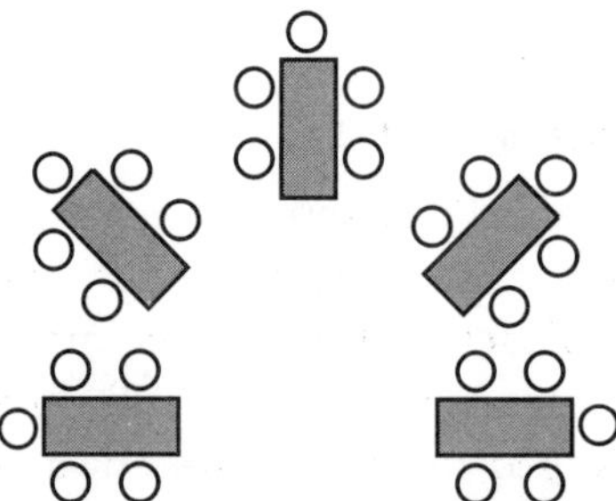

figure 1.2

2. **Team-Style:** Grouping circular or oblong tables around the classroom or grouping desks enables you to promote team interaction. Avoid putting some students with their backs to the front of the room so that they can't see you, a flip chart, board, or screen.

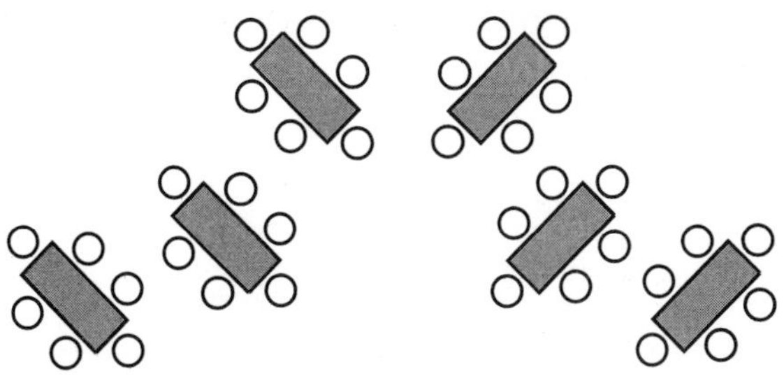

figure 1.3

3. **Conference Table:** It's best if the table is relatively circular or square. This arrangement minimizes the importance of the teacher and maximizes the importance of the class. A rectangular table often creates a sense of formality if the teacher is at the head of the table.

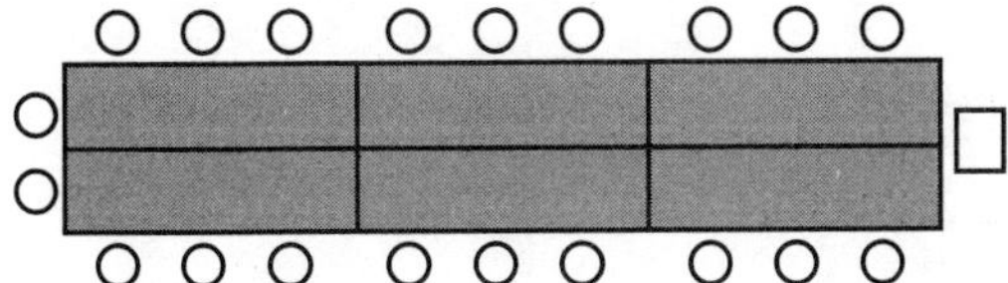

figure 1.4

If the teacher sits in the middle of a wider side, the students on the ends will feel left out.

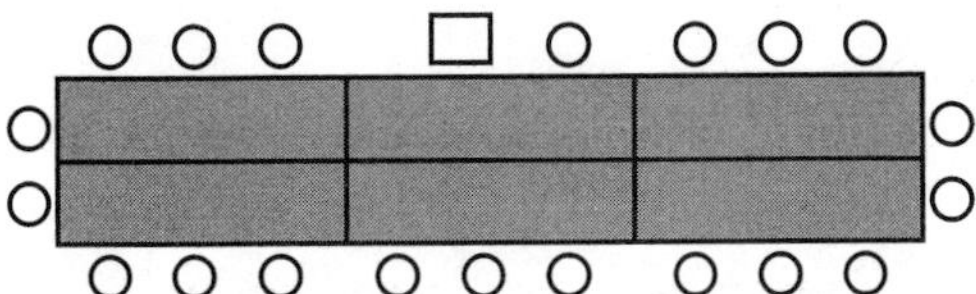

figure 1.5

You can usually form a conference table arrangement by joining several smaller tables (the center will usually be hollow).

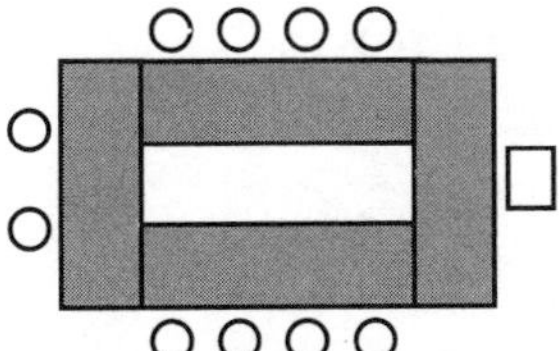

figure 1.6

4. **Circle:** Simply seating students in a circle without desks or tables promotes the most direct face-to-face interaction. A circle is ideal for full-group discussion. Assuming there is enough perimeter

space, you can ask students to arrange their chairs quickly into many subgroup arrangements.

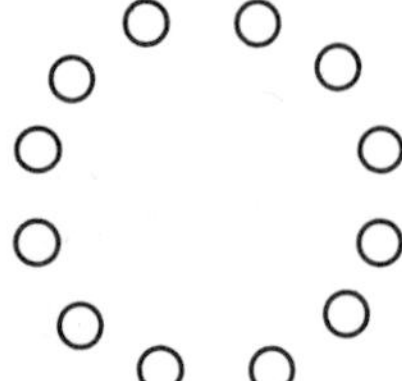

figure 1.7

If you want a writing surface available for students, use a peripheral arrangement. Have them turn their chairs around when you want group discussion.

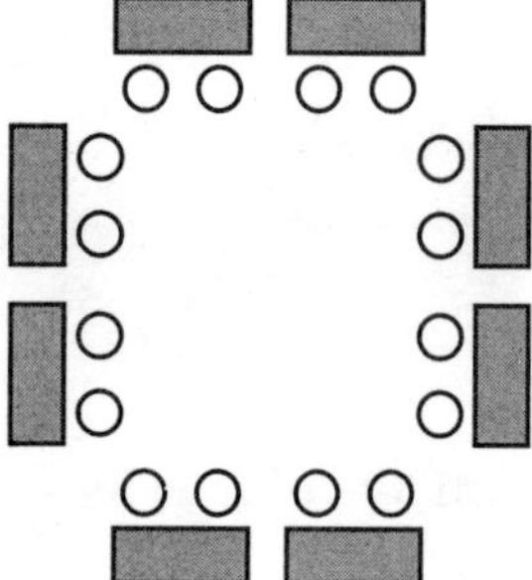

figure 1.8

5. **Traditional Classroom:** If there is no way to get around a series of straight rows of desks/tables and chairs, all is not lost. Group chairs in pairs to allow for the use of learning partners (*h̲evrutot*). Try to create an even number of rows and enough space between them so that pairs of students in the odd-number rows can turn their chairs around and create a quartet with the pair seated directly behind them in the next row.

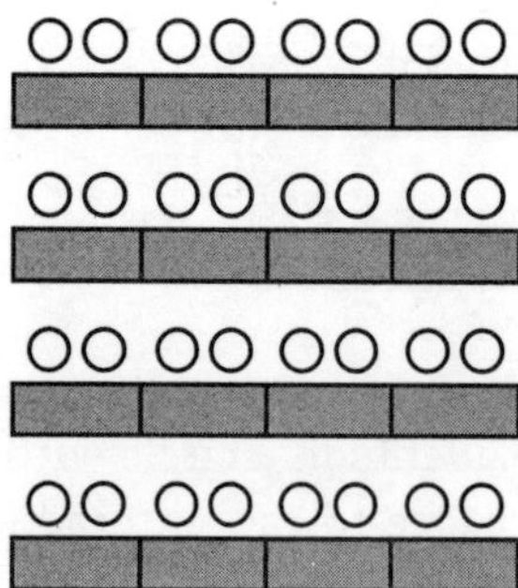

figure 1.9

You can even make do in a fixed-seat auditorium, such as a synagogue sanctuary. Ask students to seat themselves as close to the center as possible. Be assertive about this request; even consider cordoning off sections of the auditorium. Remember: No matter how large the auditorium or the size of the audience, you can pair up students and use active learning activities that involve partners.

Methods to Get Participation at Any Time

Active learning cannot occur without student participation. There are a variety of ways to structure discussion and obtain responses from students at any time during a class. Some are especially suitable when time is limited or participation needs to be coaxed. You might also consider combining these methods. For example, you might use sub-discussion and then invite a spokesperson from each group to serve on a panel.

1. **Open discussion**: Ask a question and open it up to the entire group without any further structuring. The straightforward quality of open discussion is appealing. If you are worried that the discussion might be too lengthy, say beforehand, "I'd like to ask four or five students to share..." To encourage students to raise their hands, ask, "How many of you have a response to my question?" Then call on all of the hands that are raised.

2. **Response cards**: Pass out index cards and request anonymous answers to your questions. Have the index cards passed around the group or otherwise distributed. Use response cards to save time or to provide anonymity for personally threatening self-disclosures. The need to state your views concisely on a card is another advantage of this method.

3. **Polling**: Develop a survey-like question and verbally poll students. Use polling to obtain responses quickly and in a quantifiable form. You can add interest to the survey by obtaining responses in fun ways. For example, instead of asking students to simply raise their hands, have them raise both hands (or put two thumbs up) if their feelings are very strong. You can also ask them to fold their arms if they are not sure of their opinion. Finally, they can put one or two thumbs down in disagreement. Another technique is to ask students to move out of their seats and go to a corner of the classroom

that represents their response (e.g., "strongly agree," "agree," "disagree," and "strongly disagree" corners). A variation of this idea is to request that students take seats according to their opinions. In a large classroom, for example, students who agree with a statement can get up and sit on the left side of the room, while students who disagree can sit on the right side. Students who are unsure can sit in a middle section.

4. **Learning partners (*hevrutot*)**: Have students work on tasks or discuss key questions with a student seated next to them. Use learning partners when you want to involve everybody but don't have enough time for small-group discussion. A pair is a good group configuration for developing a supportive relationship and/or for working on complex activities that would not lend themselves to large-group configurations.

5. **Subgroup discussion**: Break students into subgroups of three or four to share (and record) information. Use subgroup discussion when you have sufficient time to let students settle into small-group learning. This is one of the key methods for obtaining everyone's participation.

6. **Go-arounds**: Go around the group and obtain short responses to key questions. Use go-arounds when you want to obtain something quickly from each student. Sentence stems (e.g., "One change I would make in the Siddur is...") are useful in conducting go-arounds. Invite students to pass when they wish. Avoid repetition, if you want, by asking each student for a new contribution to the process.

7. **Panels**: Invite a small number of students to present their views in front of the entire class. An informal panel can be created by asking for the views of a designated number of students who remain in their seats. Use panels, when time permits, to have a focused, serious response to your questions. Rotate panelists to increase participation.

8. **Fishbowl**: Ask a portion of the class to form a discussion circle, and have the remaining students form a listening circle around them. Bring new groups into the inner circle to continue the discussion. Use fishbowls to help bring focus to large-group discussions. Although time consuming, this is the best method for combining

the virtues of large- and small-group discussions. As a variation to concentric circles, you can have students remain seated at a table and invite different tables or parts of a table to be the discussants as the others listen.

9. **Games**: Use a fun exercise or a quiz game to elicit students' ideas, knowledge, or skill. For example, TV game shows such as "Who Wants to Be a Millionaire?" can be used as the basis of a game that elicits active participation. Use games to pick up energy and involvement (but don't foster too much individual competition).
10. **Calling on the next speaker**: Ask students to raise their hands when they want to share their views, and request that the present speaker in the class call on the next speaker (rather than the teacher performing this role). You can have a student toss a ball or pass an object such as a toy microphone. Use calling on the next speaker when you are sure there is a lot of interest in the discussion/activity and you wish to promote student-to-student interaction.

Assignments to Give Learning Partners (*Hevrutot*)

Although we have just looked at ten ways to obtain student participation, the use of learning partners or *hevrutot* deserves special notice. One of the most effective and efficient ways to promote active learning is to divide a class into pairs and compose learning partnerships. It's hard to get left out in a pair. It's also hard to hide in one. Learning partnerships can be short- or long-term. Learning partners can undertake a wide variety of quick tasks or more time-consuming assignments, such as those in the list below.

1. **Discuss** a short written document together.
2. **Interview** each other concerning a partner's reactions to something he or she read, a lecture he or she heard, a film he or she watched, or any other educational activity.
3. **Correct or give feedback** about each other's work.
4. **Question** a partner about an assigned reading.
5. **Recap** a lesson or class session together.
6. **Develop** questions together to ask the teacher.
7. **Test** each other.
8. **Respond** to a question posed by the teacher.

Strategies to Group Students

Small-group work is a significant part of active learning. It's important to form groups quickly and efficiently, and at the same time vary the composition and sometimes the size of the groups throughout the class. The following options are interesting alternatives to letting students choose their own groups or counting off up to a number you have designated.

1. **Grouping cards**: Determine how many students are in the class and how many different groupings you want throughout the session. For example, in a class of twenty, one activity may call for four groups of five; another, five groups of four; still another, six groups of three with two observers. You will code these groups using a colored dot (red, blue, green, yellow for four groups), decorative stickers (five different stickers in a common theme for five groups—e.g., lions, monkeys, tigers, giraffes, elephants), and a Hebrew number (*eẖad* through *sheish* for six groups) or letter (*alef, bet,* or *gimmel* for three groups). Randomly place a number, colored dot, and sticker on a card for each student and include the card in the student's materials. When you are ready to form your groups, identify which code you are using and direct the students to join their groups in designated places. Students will be able to move quickly to their groups, saving time and eliminating confusion. You may want to post signs indicating group meeting areas to make the process even more efficient.

2. **Puzzles**: Purchase children's jigsaw puzzles or create your own by cutting out pictures from magazines, pasting them on cardboard, and cutting them into your desired shape, size, and number. Select the number of puzzle pieces according to the number of groups you want to create. Separate the puzzles, mix up the pieces, and give each student a puzzle piece. When you are ready to form your groups, instruct students to locate those with the pieces to complete a puzzle.

3. **Finding famous people**: Create a list of famous people who belong together in groups of three or four (examples: Mordecai, Esther, Haman, and Vashti; Moses, Miriam, Aaron, Yoẖeved; Ruth, Boaz, Naomi). Choose the same number of famous people as there are students. Write the names on index cards, one on each card, to create a group of cards. Shuffle or mix up the cards and give each

student a card with a famous name. When you are ready to form groups, ask the students to find the other members of their group. Once the famous group is complete, they are to find a spot to congregate.

4. **Name tags**: Use name tags of different shapes and/or colors to designate different groupings.

5. **Birthdays**: Ask students to line up by birthdays, then break into the number of groups you need for a particular activity. In large classes, form groups by birth months. For example, up to sixty students can be divided into three roughly equal-size groups by composing groups of those born in 1) January, February, March and April; 2) May, June, July, and August; and 3) September, October, November, and December.

Alternatives in Selecting Group Leaders and Filling Other Jobs

One of the ways to facilitate active learning in small groups is to assign jobs to some of the group members, such as **leader, timekeeper, recorder, spokesperson,** *or* **materials manager**. Often it works fine to ask for volunteers to assume some of these responsibilities. Sometimes it's fun and efficient to use a creative selection strategy.

1. **Alphabetical assignment**: Identify the jobs needed. Assign jobs in alphabetical order by first name. In a long-term group, rotate jobs using this order.

2. **Birthday assignment**: Make assignments in chronological order by students' birthdays (in the calendar year). In a long-term group, rotate jobs using this order.

3. **Number lottery**: Ask group members to count off. Place the numbers held by group members in a hat and pick the person for the job.

4. **Color lottery**: Select a color for each assignment. The person who is wearing that color receives that assignment.

5. **Pet lovers**: Assign a designated job to the person with the greatest number of pets.

Tips When Facilitating Discussion

Class discussion plays a vital role in active learning. Hearing a wide variety of views challenges students' thinking. Your role during a group discussion is to facilitate the flow of comments from students. Although it is not necessary to interject after each student speaks, periodically assisting the group with their contributions can be helpful. Here is a facilitation menu to use as you lead group discussions.

1. **Paraphrase** what someone has said so that the student feels understood and the other students can hear a concise summary of what's been said at greater length.

   So what you're saying is that you have to be very careful about the words you use because a particular person might be embarrassed by them.

2. **Check** your understanding against the words of a student or ask a student to clarify what he or she is saying.

   Are you saying that it's okay to let a person know you are really angry at him or her?

3. **Compliment** an interesting or insightful comment.

   That's a good point. I'm glad that you brought that to our attention.

4. **Elaborate** on a student's contribution to the discussion with examples or suggest a new way to view the problem.

   What you said could be true even if you were not someone's best friend.

5. **Energize** a discussion by quickening the pace, using humor, or, if necessary, prodding the group for more contributions.

   Oh, my, we have lots of quiet people in this class! Here's a challenge for you. For the next two minutes, let's see how many ideas we can come up with to make a Passover seder more lively and fun.

6. **Disagree** (gently) with a student's comments to stimulate further discussion.

   I can see where you are coming from, but I'm not sure that what you are describing is always the case. Has anyone had an experience that is different than Jake's?

7. **Mediate** differences of opinion between students and relieve any tensions that may be brewing.

   I think that Shoshana and Adina are not really disagreeing with each other but are just emphasizing two different sides of this issue.

8. **Pull together** ideas, showing their relationship to each other.

   As you can see from Daniel's and Chaya's comments, the words we use can hurt people. Both of them have given us an example of when they felt excluded by other kids.

9. **Change** the group process by altering the method for obtaining participation or moving the group to a stage of evaluating ideas that have been placed before the group.

   Let's break into smaller groups and see if you can come up with some reasons why God allows good people to suffer.

10. **Summarize** (and record, if desired) the major views of the group.

    I have noted three major ideas that have come from the group's discussion as to when words are harmful: a) they exclude some people; 2) they hurt some people; 3) they are copied by others.

Timesavers When Active Learning Takes Time

Whatever methods you use, active learning takes time. Therefore, it's crucial that no time is wasted. Many teachers, however, lose control of time by allowing a number of time wasters to occur. Here are things you can do to save time.

1. **Start on time.** This act sends a message to latecomers that you're serious. In the event that all of the students are not yet in the room, begin the class, if you wish, with a discussion or enrichment activity for which complete attendance is not absolutely necessary.
2. **Give clear instructions.** Don't start an activity when students are confused about what to do. If the directions are complicated, put them in writing.
3. **Prepare visual information ahead of time.** Don't write key ideas or directions on the board while students watch. Do it in advance.
4. **Distribute materials and worksheets quickly.** Put them in prepared packets or distribute packets to key areas of the classroom so that several people can assist with their distribution.

5. **Quicken the pace of activities from time to time.** Often, putting students under time pressure energizes them and makes them more productive.
6. **Get the class's prompt attention.** Use a variety of cues (fingers against lips) or attention-getting devices (a bell) to inform the class that you are ready to reconvene them after a small-group activity.

Interventions When Students Get Out of Hand

Using active learning techniques tends to minimize the classroom management problems that often plague teachers who rely too heavily on traditional methods. Nonetheless, difficulties such as monopolizing, distracting, and withdrawing behaviors still may occur. Below are interventions you can use. Some work well with individual students while others work with the entire class.

1. **Signal nonverbally**. Make eye contact with or move closer to students when they hold private conversations, start to fall asleep, or hide from participation. Press your fingers together (unobtrusively) to signal a wordy student to finish what they are saying. Make a T sign with your fingers to stop unwanted behavior.
2. **Listen actively**. When students monopolize discussion, go off on a tangent, or argue with you, interject with a summary of their views and then ask others to speak. Or acknowledge the value of their viewpoints, or invite them to discuss their views with you during a break.
3. **Get your ducks in a row.** When the same students speak up in class while others hold back, pose a question or problem and then ask how many people have a response to it. You should see new hands go up. Call on one of them. The same technique might work when trying to obtain volunteers for role-playing.
4. **Invoke participation rules.** From time to time, tell students that you would like to use rules such as:
   - No laughing at other students making mistakes.
   - Only students who have not spoken as yet can participate.
   - Build on one another's ideas.
   - Speak for yourself, not for others.

5. **Connect on a personal level.** Whether the problem students are hostile or withdrawn, make a point of getting to know them during breaks. It's unlikely that students will continue to give you a hard time or remain distant if you've taken an interest in them.

6. **Change the method of participation.** Sometimes you can control the damage done by difficult students by inserting new formats, such as using pairs or small groups rather than full-class activities.

7. **Discuss very negative behaviors in private.** You must call a stop to behaviors you find detrimental to learning. Firmly request, in private, a change in behavior of those students who are disruptive. If the entire class is involved, stop the lesson and explain clearly how you want students to behave.

SECTION 2 How to Get Students Active from the Start

As you begin any class, it is critical to get students active from the start. If you don't, you run the risk that passivity will set in, much like cement that has had time to dry. Structure opening activities that get students to become acquainted, move about, engage their minds, and focus their interest on the subject matter. These experiences can sometimes be considered as the "appetizers" to a full meal. They allow students to get a taste of what is to follow. Although some teachers choose to begin a class with a short introduction, adding at least one opening exercise to your teaching plan is a first step that has many benefits. Let us explore why.

Starting Goals

In the earliest moments of the school year there are two important goals to accomplish. These goals are:

1. **Getting acquainted**—helping students to become acquainted with one another and creating a spirit of cooperation and interdependence.
2. **Immediate learning involvement**—creating initial interest in the subject matter.

Both goals, when accomplished, help to develop a learning environment that involves students, promotes their willingness to take part in some active learning, and creates positive classroom norms. As little as five minutes or as much as two hours for opening activities (depending on the overall length of your class) will be time well spent. Reintroducing these activities from time to time throughout a course of study also helps to renew team building, and rebuild interest in the subject matter.

In this chapter we will examine strategies for accomplishing these two goals. You should find several that will work for you.

As you select opening strategies to use in your class, keep in mind the following considerations.

1. **Level of threat**: Is the class that you are teaching open to new ideas and activities, or do you anticipate hesitation and reservation from students in the beginning? Opening with a strategy that exposes students' lack of knowledge or skill can be risky; they may not be ready to reveal their limitations. Alternatively, a strategy that asks students to comment on something familiar to them eases their involvement in the class.
2. **Appropriateness to student norms**: A class of adolescents may be initially less accepting of playing games than a group of fifth graders. Girls may feel more comfortable sharing their feelings in a self-disclosure exercise than boys. You are setting the stage for the entire class as you select an opening activity; consider your students and plan appropriately.
3. **Relevance to the subject matter**: Unless you are interested in a simple exchange of names, the strategies you are about to read offer an excellent opportunity for students to begin learning course material. Alter a suggested icebreaker so that it reflects the material that you are planning to teach in your course. The closer the tie-in of your exercise to your subject matter, the easier transition you will be able to make to the major learning activities you have in store.

These considerations have relevance for every aspect of your course of instruction, yet they are especially important in the opening stages. A successful opening sets the tone for a successful class. Likewise, one that seems threatening, silly, or unrelated to the rest of your course can create an awkward atmosphere that is difficult to overcome.

Getting to Know You

The first set of strategies helps students to get acquainted and reacquainted or to build team spirit with a group that already knows one another. These strategies also promote an active learning environment by getting students to move physically, to share openly their opinions and feelings, and to accomplish something in which they can take pride. Many of these strategies are well known throughout the teaching profession. Some are our own original creations. All of them get students active from the start.

When you use these team-building strategies, try to relate them to the subject matter of your class. Experiment with ones new to you and your students. In today's world, students are so accustomed to certain popular icebreakers that they may be turned off to them rather than turned on by them. They will welcome activities that are refreshingly different.

1 • Who's in the Class?

Overview

This popular icebreaker is a scavenger hunt for classmates rather than for objects. The hunt can be designed in a number of ways and for any size class. It fosters team building and gets physical movement right at the beginning of a class.

Procedure

1. Devise six to ten descriptive statements to complete the phrase: ***Find someone who...***

   Include statements that identify personal information and/or class ontent. Use some of these beginnings:

   Find someone who...

   likes/enjoys ______________________.
   knows what a ______________________ is.
   thinks that ______________________.
   is good at ______________________.
   has already ______________________.
   is motivated by ______________________.
   believes that ______________________.
   has recently read a book about ______________________.
   has experience with ______________________.
   dislikes ______________________.
   has previously learned ______________________.
   has a great idea for ______________________.
   owns a ______________________.

wants or doesn't want ______________________ .
has the same ____________________________ .

2. Distribute the statements to students and give the following instructions:
"This activity is like a scavenger hunt, except that you are looking for people instead of objects. When I say 'begin,' circulate around the room looking for people who match these statements. You can only use a person for one statement, even if he or she matches more than one. When you have found a match, write down the person's first name."
3. When most students have finished, call a stop to the hunt and reconvene the full class.
4. You may want to offer a token prize to the person who finishes first. More important, survey the class about each of the items. Promote short discussions of some of the items that might stimulate interest in the class topic.

Variations

1. Avoid competition entirely by giving the scavenger hunt enough time to allow everyone to complete it (as far as possible).
2. Ask students to meet others and find out how many matches can be made with each person.
3. Younger students can do this activity without a sheet. Give them one oral instruction—e.g., "Find someone who has the same number of brothers and sisters as you." Let them find the match and exchange names. Encourage them to meet different students for each round.
4. Have fewer questions (five or six) and allow more time for reviewing the information.

Example

Who in the class...

1. was born in the same month as you? ________________________
2. has ever been to Israel (or wants to visit Israel)? ____________

3. is familiar with the *Mah Tovu* prayer? ____________________

4. likes to eat *hallah*?____________________

5. enjoys celebrating Purim? ____________________

6. can sing the *Shema* by heart? ____________________

7. has the same English or Hebrew name as you? ____________________

8. has been to a camp? ____________________

9. dislikes broccoli?____________________

10. wants to read Hebrew faster?____________________

2. Predictions

Overview

This is a fascinating way to help students become acquainted with one another. It also is an interesting experiment in first impressions that may help you in learning about your students.

Procedure

1. Form small groups of three or four students (who are relative strangers to one another).
2. Tell students that their job is to predict how each person in their group would answer certain questions you have prepared for them. Below are some all-purpose possibilities.
   - What type of music do you enjoy?
   - What are some of your favorite hobbies or activities?
   - How many hours a day do you usually play video games?
   - How many siblings do you have, and where are you in the sibling order?
   - What is your favorite Jewish food?
   - What is your favorite Jewish holiday (or prayer, or song, or biblical character)?

   Note: Other questions can be added or substituted depending on the students in your class.
3. Have the small groups begin by selecting one person as the first subject. Urge group members to be as specific as possible in their predictions about that person. Tell them not to be afraid of bold guesses! As they guess, request the subject to give no indication as to the accuracy of the predictions attempted. When others fin-

ish their predictions about the subject, he or she should reveal the answer to each question about him or herself.

4. Have each group member take a turn as the focus person.

Variations

1. Create questions that require students to make predictions about one another's views and beliefs (rather than factual information). For example, ask, "What's the most important quality a friend should have?"
2. Eliminate the predictions. Instead, invite students one by one to answer the questions immediately. Then ask small-group members to reveal what facts about each other surprised them (based on their first impressions).

Examples

1. If you are about to study Passover, you could ask students to predict how fellow students would answer these questions:
   - Who hides the *afikomen* at your family seder? An adult? The kids?
   - Do you like to eat *maror*?
   - Which song do you like the most at the seder?
   - Do you think the wicked child is really a bad person?

   Ask younger students to guess how their classmates would answer these questions:
   - What holiday do you like the best?
   - Do you like latkes better than noodle kugel?
   - Did you ever dress up as Haman for Purim?
   - What is your favorite Jewish song?

3. Advertising Slogans

Overview

This is an excellent opener for students who already know one another. It can produce rapid team building.

Procedure

1. Divide students into teams of no more than six members.
2. Ask teams to create a slogan (e.g., "Better Living Through Torah") that advertises the subject of the class, such as its value to them or to the world.
3. Before each team begins planning its advertising slogan, give them a list of advertising slogans that are currently popular as a guide. You can also give them popular expressions ("A penny saved is a penny earned"). Invite them to use words from one of these slogans or expressions, if they wish.
4. Ask each team to present its slogan. Praise everyone's creativity.

Variation

Students can create ad slogans for their class, their synagogue, or anything else of which they are proud.

Examples

1. *Lashon ha-Ra*...just say no.
2. *Hamentashen*...you can't stop after eating just one!
3. *Shul* on *Shabbat* is cool.
4. *Latkes*...try them; you'll like them.
5. A house is not a home without a *mezzuzah*.

6. *Keeping kosher...* just do it.
7. *The Torah...* it's priceless.
8. *Tzedakah* starts at home.
9. With a name like *Deuteronomy*, it's got to be good.
10. A life saved is a *mitzvah* earned.

4. The Company You Keep

Overview

This activity introduces physical movement right from the start and helps students to get acquainted. It moves rapidly and is a lot of fun.

Procedure

1. Make a list of categories you think might be appropriate for a getting-acquainted activity for the class you are teaching. All-purpose categories include:
   - The month in which you were born
   - People who like/don't like (identify a preference, such as acting in a play)
   - Your favorite (identify any item, such as book, song, TV program)
   - The hand with which you write
   - The color of your shoes
   - Agreement or disagreement with any statement of opinion on a current issue (e.g., "Global warming is very real").

   You can also use categories that relate directly to the subject matter you are teaching, such as:
   - Favorite Jewish holiday, food, prayer, or biblical character
   - People who agree/disagree that (identify an issue related to your class topic)
   - People who know/don't know who or what (identify a person or concept related to your class topic) is
2. Clear some floor space so that students can move around freely.

3. Call out a category. Direct students to locate, as quickly as possible, all the people who they would associate with, given the category. For example, right-handers and left-handers would separate into two groups. Or those who agree with a statement would separate from those who disagree. If the category contains more than two choices (e.g., the month of students' birthdays), ask students to congregate with those like them, thereby forming several groups.
4. When students form the appropriate clusters, ask them to shake hands with the company they keep. Invite all to observe approximately how many people there are in different groups.
5. Proceed immediately to the next category. Keep the students moving from group to group as you announce new categories.
6. Reconvene the entire class. Discuss the diversity of students revealed by the exercise.

Variations

1. Ask students to locate someone who is different from them rather than the same. For example, you might ask students to find someone who has a different eye color. (Whenever there are not equal numbers of students in different categories, allow more than one person from one group to cluster with someone from another group.)
2. Invite students to suggest categories.

Examples

Get into a group of those in the class who...

1. have the same favorite Jewish holiday as you.
2. are wearing the same color shirt as you.
3. prefer soccer, football, baseball, or basketball.
4. think that parents should monitor a kid's internet use.
5. like their English name.
6. have Hebrew names that begins with the same letter as yours.
7. believe that God is a He? She? Neither?
8. will become a bar or bat mitzvah in the same month as you.

5. • Really Getting Acquainted

Overview

Most getting-acquainted activities are limited opportunities to get to meet others. An alternative is to arrange an in-depth experience in which pairs of students can become really well acquainted. This is especially helpful when students come from different towns or secular schools.

Procedure

1. Pair up students in any manner you desire. Criteria for pairing up students might include:
   - two students who have never met before
   - two students who have never worked together
   - two students who come from different neighborhoods or towns
2. Ask pairs that are formed to spend two to ten minutes getting to know each other. (The older the students, the more time you might provide.)
3. Supply some questions that students can use to interview each other.
4. When the entire class reconvenes, give pairs a task to do together that enables them to start learning about the subject matter of the class (see "Assignments to Give Learning Partners," page xx).
5. Consider the appropriateness of transforming the pairs into long-term learning partnerships.

Variations

1. Form trios or quartets instead of pairs.

2. Have students introduce their partners to the entire class.

Examples

Here are some interview questions you might use:

1. Did you always live in this community?
2. Who is in your family?
3. What's your favorite subject in school? Your least favorite subject?
4. What do you like to do when you have free time?
5. What's your favorite TV program, CD, video game?
6. Do you watch the news?
7. What do you think needs to change in our country? Our world?
8. What makes you proud to be Jewish?
9. Do you know someone who is humble? Courageous?
10. In what way do you believe people are God's partners?

6. The Shofar Blows

Overview

This is a fast-paced icebreaker that gets students moving and laughing. It's a good team builder and allows students to get to know each other.

Procedure

1. Arrange a circle of chairs. Ask each student to sit on one of the chairs. There should be exactly enough chairs for all students.
2. Tell the students that if they agree with your next statement, they should stand up and move to another chair.

   Stand in the center of the circle and say, "My name is ________, and THE SHOFAR BLOWS for everybody who..." Choose an ending that would likely apply to nearly everyone in the class, such as "likes chocolate ice cream."
3. At this point, everyone who likes chocolate ice cream gets up and runs to another empty chair. As the students move, make sure you occupy one of the empty seats. If you do, then one student will have no seat to occupy and will replace you as the person in the center.
4. Have the new person in the center finish the same incomplete sentence: "My name is __________, and THE SHOFAR BLOWS for everybody who..." with a new ending. It can be humorous (e.g., "still sleeps with a night light") or serious (e.g., "who is worried about Israel's security").
5. Play the game as often as seems appropriate.

Variations

1. Provide an extensive list of endings that the students can use. Include material relevant to the subject matter of the class (e.g., "prefers *latkes* to *hamentashen*") or to the life experience of the students ("finds taking tests stressful").
2. Have pairs of students in the center instead of just one child. Invite them to jointly select an appropriate ending for the sentence.

Examples

Here are endings you might use:

- stays up too late
- does not like homework
- would rather start school at 10:00 a.m. and end at 4:30 p.m.
- would prefer that religious school be held on one day of the weekend from 9:00 a.m.–1:00 p.m.
- likes peanut butter
- enjoys video games
- thinks protecting the environment is *very* important
- knows what the word *havdalah* means
- believes that when one becomes bar or bat mitzvah these days the party is emphasized more than the service/ceremony
- went to the nursery school at this synagogue[1]
- is proud to be Jewish

[1]Suggested by Ellen Walters.

7. Instant Assessment

Overview

This is a fun, non-threatening strategy to get to know your students. You can use it to assess instantly students' backgrounds, experiences, attitudes, expectations, and concerns.

Procedure

1. Create a set of responder cards for each student. These cards could contain the letters A, B, or C for multiple-choice questions, T or F for true/false questions, or numerical ratings such as 1–5. (If it is too time-consuming to make the cards in advance, have students create their own cards on the spot.) Another way to do this is to distribute two to three index cards per student, each in a different color.
2. Develop a set of statements that students can respond to with one of their cards. Here is an example for each type of responder card mentioned above.

   I am becoming a bar/bat mitzvah because:

   a. my parents insist that I do it.

   b. I am really interested in having this experience.

   c. it's a wonderful way for my family to celebrate.

   I am concerned that becoming a bar/bat mitzvah will be difficult for me.

   - True or false?

I believe that becoming a bar/bat mitzvah will be useful to me in the future.

1	2	3	4	5
strongly disagree				strongly agree

You can create similar statements about your students' knowledge, attitudes, and experiences.

3. Read the first statement and ask students to answer by holding up the card of their choice.
4. Quickly assess the audience response. Invite a few students to share the reasons for their choices.
5. Continue with the remaining statements.

Variations

1. Instead of using cards, ask younger students to stand when their choice is announced.
2. Use a conventional show of hands, but add interest by encouraging students to raise both hands when they strongly agree with a response.
3. Use picture cards with younger students.[2]

Examples

1. The most important subject in religious school is...
   yellow card—Hebrew
   blue card—Bible
   pink card—holidays
2. I feel happy and proud to be Jewish when...
   yellow card—everyone joins in the singing of *Hatikvah*.
   blue card—everyone sings *Simon Tov and Mazal Tov* at a bar/bat mitzvah service or wedding.
   pink card—everyone sings *Etz Chaim Hee* before closing the ark.
3. The most important Jewish ritual object is...
   yellow card—the *Hanukkah* menorah

[2]From *Tiku Shofar*, p. 8.

blue card—*Shabbat* candles

pink card—the *mezzuzah*

4. If you could interview someone, it would be...

   yellow card—Miriam when she led the women in a great dance upon crossing the Red Sea

   blue card—Moses when he received the Ten Commandments

   pink card—Ben Gurion at the proclamation of the State of Israel in 1948

5. The person who did the most for the Jewish people is...

   yellow card—Queen Esther

   blue card—Albert Einstein

   pink card—Abraham

6. My favorite Jewish song is...

   yellow card—*Hava Nagillah*

   blue card—*L'kha Dodi*

   pink card—Light One Candle

Immediate Learning Involvement

Yet another way to get students active from the start is to utilize the strategies that follow. They are designed to plunge students immediately into the subject matter in order to build their interest, arouse their curiosity, and stimulate thinking. After all, what good are students if their brains (or, if you will, their "computers") are *not on?* Many teachers make the mistake of teaching too early, before students are engaged and mentally ready. Using any of these strategies will correct that tendency.

8. Active Knowledge Sharing

Overview: This is a great way to draw students immediately into the subject matter of your course. You can also use it to assess the knowledge level of students and at the same time do some team building. It works with any class and with any subject matter.

Procedure

1. Provide a list of questions pertaining to the subject matter you will be teaching. It is a good idea to include questions on various levels to insure that everyone will be able to answer at least some of the questions and that the more knowledgeable students will be challenged as well. You could include some or all of the following categories:
   - Words to define (e.g., "What is *tashlich*?")
   - Multiple-choice questions concerning facts or concepts (e.g., "Moses was born in: a. Canaan, b. Egypt, c. Midian")
   - People to identify (e.g., "Who is Theodore Herzl?")
   - Questions concerning actions one could take in certain situations (e.g., "What *bracha* do you say when you are about to eat cake?")
   - Incomplete sentences (e.g., " __________is the second book of the Torah.")
2. Ask students to answer the questions as well as they can in the time you provide.
3. Then invite them to mill around the room, finding others who can answer questions they do not know how to answer or can improve their own answers. Encourage students to help one another. If you are concerned that one or two students will be giving all the answers, have a rule that students may only share one or two answers with each student.

4. Reconvene the full class and review the answers. Fill in answers unknown to the students. Use the information as a way to introduce topics of importance in the class or to introduce a new unit of study.

Variations

1. Hand out an index card to each student. Ask students to write down one piece of information they are sure is accurate concerning the subject matter of the class. Invite the students to mill around, sharing what they wrote on their cards. Encourage them to write down new information garnered from other students. As a full group, review the information collected.
2. Use opinion questions rather than factual ones, or mix factual questions with opinion questions.

Examples

ACTIVE KNOWLEDGE SHARING: THE *AMIDAH*

1. When we recite the *Amidah*, why do we stand with our feet together and at attention? (to show proper respect)
2. We bow during the *Amidah* when we say:
   a. (beginning of first blessing of *Amidah*)
   b. (end of first blessing of *Amidah*)
   c. (beginning of *modim anahnu lakh*)
   d. (end of *modim anahnu lack*)
3. The word *Amidah* means:
   a. The Eighteen Blessings
   b. The Holy Prayer
   c. The Standing Prayer
4. What does it mean to pray the *Amidah* with *kavanah*? (intention, deep feeling)
5. In what way is the Shabbat *Amidah* different from the weekday *Amidah*? (It does not have requests of God)
6. True or false? You may add your own blessing at the end of the *Amidah*. (True, but not in the traditional format.)

7. Why do you think that we begin the *Amidah* by mentioning our ancestors? (to remind God of God's relationship to our ancestors [*z'khut*] and to remind us of our heritage)

ACTIVE KNOWLEDGE SHARING: HIGH HOLIDAYS

1. What's "high" about the High Holidays? (spiritual and holy)
2. Why do we have honey on *Rosh ha-Shanah*? (sweet new year)
3. What prayer do we say when we dip the *hallah* into the honey? (*sh'tikhasesh aleinu shana tova um'tukah*)
4. The Hebrew name for the High Holidays is ____ . (*Yamin Noraim)*
5. True or false? *Yom Kippur* comes seven days after *Rosh ha-Shanah.* (False; 10 days)
6. What are Jews expected to do between *Rosh ha-Shanah* and *Yom Kippur?* (seek forgiveness from God and people we have wronged)

9. Rotating Trios

Overview

This is an in-depth way for students to discuss issues with some (but usually not all) of their classmates. The exchanges can easily be geared to the subject matter of any class.

Procedure

1. Compose a variety of questions that help students begin discussion of the topic. Use questions with no right or wrong answers.
2. Divide students into trios. Place trios in the room so that each trio can clearly see a trio to its right and to its left. The overall configuration of the trios would be a circle or square.
3. Give each trio an opening question (the same question for each trio) to discuss. Select the least challenging question you have devised to begin the trio exchange. Suggest that each person in the trio take a turn answering the question.
4. After a suitable period of discussion, ask the trios to assign a 0, 1, or 2 to each of its members. Direct the students with the number 1 to rotate one trio clockwise. Ask the students with the number 2 to rotate two trios clockwise. Ask the students with the number 0 to remain seated, since they are permanent members of a trio site. Have them raise their hands high so that rotating students can find them. The result will be entirely new trios.
5. Start a new exchange with a new question. Increase the difficulty of the questions as you proceed to new rounds.
6. You can rotate trios as many times as you have questions to pose and discussion time to allot. Use the same rotation procedure each

time. For example, in a trio exchange of three rotations, each student will get to meet six other students in depth.

Variations

1. After each round of questions, quickly poll the full group about their responses before rotating students to new trios.
2. Use pairs or quartets instead of trios. Pairs are easier for younger students. One could be the *alef* partner and the other the *bet* partner. The *bet* students could move one place ahead after each round while the *alef* students stay in place.
3. Give each student in the original trio a different color card. Have the students rotate by color. For example, students with blue stay, students with yellow move one trio, and students with green move two trios.

Examples

Seder

Round 1: Ask the students what they like about a seder.

Round 2: Ask students what they think is the most important part of the seder and why.

Round 3: Ask students what they think would make a seder better.

Prayer

Round 1. Ask students why many think the *Shema* is the most important Jewish prayer.

Round 2. Ask students why the *Shema* begins with "Hear".

Round 3. Ask students what the *Shema* says to them personally.

Israel

Round 1. Ask students why they think Israel is important in the history of the Jewish people.

Round 2. Ask students what role Israel plays for Jews today.

Round 3. Ask students what role Israel plays in their own lives.

10. Go to Your Choice

Overview

This is a well-known way to incorporate physical movement at the beginning of a class. This strategy is flexible enough to use for a variety of activities that are designed to stimulate initial interest in your subject matter. It can also be done as a concluding activity.

Procedure

1. For each round, post signs around the classroom that contain choices students have when answering one or more survey questions. You can use two signs to create a dichotomous choice or several signs that provide more options. (Post pictures instead of words for younger students.)
2. These signs can indicate a variety of preferences:
   - topics or skills of interest to the students (e.g., What would you rather learn about—holidays or new prayers?)
   - questions about course content (e.g., What is the most important reason for celebrating Hanukkah—the victory of the Maccabees, the miracle of the oil, or some other reason?)
   - different solutions to the same problem or situation (e.g., What helps a person most to be a good human being—having a good heart or observing religious rituals?)
   - different values (e.g., What helps the Jewish people the most—someone having money, fame, or a good family life?)
   - different well-known Jewish people in a field (e.g., Who is most responsible for the establishment of the State of Israel—Theodore Herzl, David Ben Gurion, or Henrietta Szold?)

- different quotations, proverbs, verses in a text, etc. (e.g., Which one of the Ten Commandments do you think is most important?)

3. Ask students to look at the choices and pick one. For example, some students might be more interested in learning about Jewish holidays than about history. Have them sign up for their preference by moving to the place in the classroom where their choice is posted.
4. Have the subgroups that have been created discuss among themselves why they have placed themselves by their sign. Ask a representative of each group to summarize their reasons.

Variations

1. Pair up students with different preferences and ask them to compare their views. Or create a discussion panel with representatives from each preference group.
2. Ask each preference group to make a presentation, create an advertisement, or prepare a skit that advocates their preference.

Examples:

1. When I say the *Shema*, I...
   a. proudly proclaim Judaism's monotheistic teaching.
   b. think of all the Jews who came before me and have said this.
   c. feel the connection among people, God, and nature.
2. My favorite name for a synagogue is...
   a. *Beth Shalom*
   b. The Jewish Center
   c. *Shir Ami*
   d. *Rodfei Tzedek*
3. The Torah was written by...
   a. God
   b. People

4. To which cause would you rather give *tzedakah*?
   a. Israel
   b. Meals for the elderly
   c. The Red Cross
5. Prayer is like...
   a. looking in a mirror.
   b. shopping in a supermarket.
   c. making a collage.
   d. making a phone call.
6. Which is your favorite Jewish symbol?
   a. *Magen David*
   b. Torah
   c. Menorah

11. Exchanging Viewpoints

Overview

This activity can be utilized to stimulate immediate involvement in the subject matter of your class. It also alerts students to be careful listeners and open themselves to diverse viewpoints.

Procedure

1. Give each student a name tag. Instruct students to write their name on the tag and wear it.
2. Ask students to pair off and introduce themselves to someone else. Then ask pairs to exchange their responses to a provocative question or statement that solicits their opinion about an issue concerning the subject matter you are teaching.
   - An example of a statement is: "We should follow everything in the Torah." Agree or disagree?
3. Call time and direct students to exchange name tags with their partners and then go on to meet another student. Instead of introducing themselves, students should share the views of the person who was their previous partner (the person whose name tag they are now wearing).
4. Next, ask students to switch name tags again and find others to talk to, sharing only the views of the person whose name tag they are now wearing.
5. Continue the process until most of the students have met. Then tell each student to retrieve his or her own name tag.

Variations

1. Use this name tag exchange process as a social icebreaker by instructing students to share background information about themselves rather than viewpoints about a provocative question or statement.
2. Eliminate an exchange of name tags. Instead, ask students to continue to meet new people, each time hearing their opinions about the question or statement given by you.

Examples

Provocative questions or statements:

- Is the best Jew one who lives in Israel?
- Is Orthodox Judaism the most authentic brand of Judaism?
- What is your favorite Jewish holiday?
- Is Hanukkah an important holiday for Jews today who live in America?
- Shabbat should be about spirituality, not rules. Agree? Disagree?
- Should you pray for a good grade on a math test?
- What enables people to change for the better?
- Why does the *Shema* say "hear" and not "see"?
- What should you do (according to Jewish teaching) if a street person asks you for money?
- Where does your community's *tzedakah* giving fall on Rambam's Ladder? How could it be elevated a rung or two?
- Was Esau misunderstood? Was he not such a negative character?
- Was it fair that Moses was not allowed to enter the Promised Land?

12. Preview

Overview

This technique encourages students to explore a new textbook so that they are engaged with its contents before beginning any lessons.

Procedure

1. Instead of simply handing out textbooks and asking the students to open to a particular page to begin learning, have them look through the new book to answer a number of questions.
2. Questions you might ask include:
   - What is your reaction to the table of contents or chapter titles?
   - What interests you as you turn the pages?
   - How familiar are the contents of the text to you?

Variation

Have students brainstorm their own questions. They can do this individually or with a partner. Then the whole group answers the questions.

Examples

Students are given a new textbook about Israel. You ask them to look through the book and answer questions like the following, one at a time:

1. Which picture catches your eye?
2. Find a fact that you never knew before.
3. Which chapter do you know the least about?
4. Which chapter do you know the most about?

5. Which people described in the book do you recognize?
6. Is there a topic that you think is not covered in this book that is important to study?
7. Are there any art projects (or writing projects) you think our class can do after we study a particular chapter in this book on Israel?
   Note: You may want to put a list of potential projects on the board to stimulate their thinking and generate enthusiasm (e.g., building miniature cities, map making, creating posters about wildlife, doing micrography like that done in S'fat, paper cutting, making mosaic tiles, writing journals, biographies, fictional stories, interviews, newspapers, etc.).
8. After perusing the chapter on foods eaten in Israel, ask them for ideas for a closing party or event.
9. Younger students who are given a new Hebrew book could be asked to find letters or words that they know and do not know (indicating the latter by page and line number). For a holiday, ask younger children to find pictures of holiday objects that they can identify.

13. True or False?

Overview

This collaborative activity stimulates instant involvement in the subject matter of your class. It promotes team building, knowledge sharing, and immediate learning.

Procedure

1. Compose a list of statements related to your subject matter, half of which are true and half of which are false. For example, the statement "*Heshvan* is a month without a Jewish holiday" is true, and the statement, "There can only be one month of *Adar*" is false. Write each statement on a separate index card. Make sure there are as many cards as there are students in the class.
2. Distribute one card to each student. Tell the class that their mission is to determine which cards are true and which are false. *Explain that they are free to use any method they want to accomplish the task.*
3. When the class is finished, have each card read and obtain the class's opinion about whether the statement is true or false.
4. Give feedback about each card and note the ways in which the class worked together on the assignment.
5. Indicate that the positive team skills shown will be necessary throughout this class because of the active learning it will feature.

Variations

1. Before the activity begins, recruit some students as observers. Ask them to give feedback about the quality of teamwork that emerged.

2. Instead of factual statements, create a list of opinions and place each opinion on an index card. Distribute cards and ask students to attempt to reach a consensus about student reactions to each opinion. Ask them to respect minority viewpoints.

Example

For a lesson on the Passover seder, true statements:

1. The word *seder* means order.
2. The kiddush formally begins the seder.
3. *Nirtzah* concludes the seder.
4. The youngest present asks the four questions.
5. We drink four cups of wine.
6. *Marror* means a bitter herb.

False statements:

1. There are ten parts of the seder.
2. Moses is mentioned in a traditional *Haggadah.*
3. When we drink wine or grape juice, we lean to the right.
4. Next year, we hope to celebrate Passover in California.
5. We place a kosher marshmallow on our seder plate.
6. In the song *Eẖad Mi Yodeah,* "one" stands for "one seder".

For a lesson on *Middot*, true statements:

1. *Anavah* means humility.
2. *Erekh Apayim* means slow to anger.
3. *Sh'miat ha-Ozen* means attentiveness.

False statements:

1. *Simẖah* means calmness.
2. *Emet* means a lie.
3. *Yirah* means haughtiness.

SECTION 3 How to Help Students Acquire Knowledge, Skills, and Attitudes Actively

If the strategies presented in the previous section were the appetizers for active learning, the ones to which you will soon be introduced are the entrees. Education at all levels is about acquiring *knowledge, skills,* and *attitudes.* Cognitive learning (knowledge) includes the gaining of information and concepts. It deals not only with comprehending the subject matter but also with analyzing it and applying it to new situations. Behavioral learning (skills) includes the development of students' ability to perform tasks, solve problems, and express themselves. Affective learning (attitudes) involves the examination and clarification of feelings and preferences. Students are involved in assessing themselves and their personal relationship to the subject matter. How *knowledge, skills,* and *attitudes* are acquired makes all the difference in the world. Will it be done passively or actively?

Active learning of information, skills, and attitudes occurs through a process of inquiry. Students are in a searching mode rather than a reactive one. By this we mean that they are looking for answers to questions posed to them or posed by them. They are seeking solutions to problems teachers have challenged them to solve. They are interested in obtaining information or skills to complete tasks assigned to them. And they are confronted with issues that compel them to examine what they believe and value. All this occurs when students are engaged in tasks and activities that gently push them to think, do, and feel. These kinds of activities can be created using the many strategies you will find in this section.

This section is divided into several parts.

Full-Class Learning: This part deals with ways to make teacher-led instruction more interactive. You will find strategies for presenting information and ideas that engage students mentally.

Class Discussion: This part explores ways to intensify dialogue and debate of key issues in your subject matter. You will find strategies that encourage active and widespread student participation.

Cooperative Learning: This part presents ways to design learning tasks done by small groups of students. You will find strategies that foster student cooperation and interdependence.

Affective Learning: This part pertains to ways to help students examine their feelings, values, and attitudes. You will find strategies to facilitate self-understanding, spirituality, and values clarification.

Skill Development: This part deals with the learning and practicing of skills, especially Hebrew reading and language. You will find strategies to expedite initial skill development and further practice.

Computer-mediated Learning: This part gives you ways to enhance your students' learning through the use of computers and the internet.

Full-Class Learning

The strategies in this section are designed to enhance full-class instruction. As you will read, even lecture-based lesson presentations can be made active by utilizing a variety of techniques. You will also find ways to improve the viewing of films and the appearance of guest presenters. Finally, you will find novel ways to teach difficult concepts and ideas so that student understanding is maximized.

14. • Leading Off

Overview

The purpose of this technique is to catch the interest of students at the beginning of the lesson.

Procedure

1. Select one of the following ways to lead off a lesson or discussion:
   - Display a quotation on the board that pertains to your topic.
   - Tell an interesting story (it can be a personal anecdote or a fictional tale).
   - Show a visual (e.g., cartoon or graphic) that attracts the students' attention to what you are going to teach.
2. After this experience, make a transition from the leadoff to the main body of the lesson. For example, you can use the quotation, story, or visual to introduce students to a topic, get them curious about a topic, or develop personal connections to the topic.

Variation

From your leadoff strategy, have the students guess what you are going to teach. This will increase their curiosity.

Examples

1. This story can be used to begin a lesson on *Rosh ha-Shanah*. It can also be used to teach the *mitzvah* of *Tzar Ba'alai Hayyim* (kindness to all living things).

WHERE WAS RABBI DAVID?[3]

Rabbi David of Lelov was the *shofar* blower at the synagogue of the great Rabbi Jacob Isaac, who was known as the Seer of Lublin. But on one *Rosh ha-Shanah,* when it was time to blow the *shofar,* Rabbi David was nowhere to be found. The Seer of Lublin sent one of the students to find him. After searching and searching he found Rabbi David in the marketplace feeding the horses. When the student scolded Rabbi David for being late, he replied, "I know that all the Jewish wagon drivers are in the synagogue today, and I was worried that they might have forgotten to feed the horses. It is a *mitzvah* to prevent cruelty to animals." They both returned to the synagogue, and Rabbi David blew the *shofar.* Then the Seer of Lublin remarked, "Today Rabbi David did a holy deed."

2. These letters to God can be used to begin a class on ideas about the nature of God and our relationship to God. Children can also be invited to write their own letters.

   Dear GOD,
   Please send me a pony. I never asked for anything before. You can look it up.—Bruce

   Dear GOD,
   Maybe Cain and Abel would not kill each other so much if they had their own rooms. It works with my brother.—Larry

   Dear GOD,
   I think the stapler is one of your best inventions.—Ruth

   Dear GOD,
   I would like to live 900 years like the guy in the Bible.—Chris

   GOD,
   We read that Thomas Edison invented light. But in religious school, they said you did it. I bet he stole your idea.—Hannah

[3]"Where Was Rabbi David" is a story composed by Shoshana Silberman in *Tiku Shofar,* United Synagogue of Conservative Judaism Commission on Jewish Education, New York, 1993. It is based on a tale about the Seer of Lublin found in *The Rosh HaShana Anthology,* Phillip Goodman, The Jewish Publication Society, 1973.

Dear GOD,
You are the one that makes miracles. You help everyone and worked so hard to make the earth and keep it alive. You made people, rainbows, the sun, moon, and stars. You made the sun to rise and set. You made all living things. Thank you so much, so very much.
Love from one of your many creations—Melissa[4]

3. As a lead visual to teaching a prayer, display graphics such as:

healing prayer

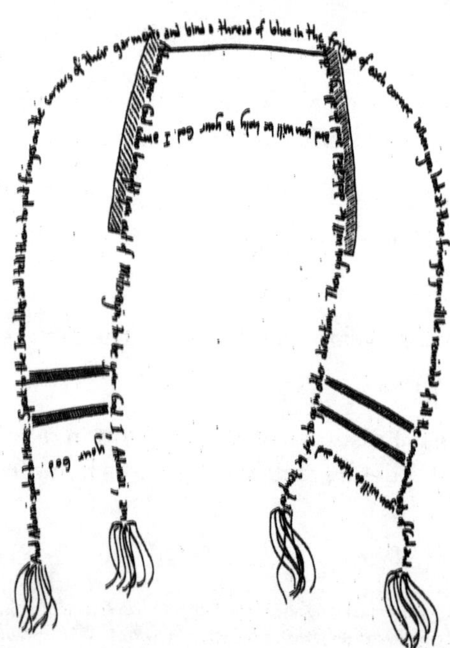

Shema[5]

Graphic by Jonathan Kremer in *Siddur Shema Israel* by Shoshana Silberman, United Synagogue of Conservative Judaism Commission on Jewish Education, New York, 1996. Reprinted with permission.

4. As an introduction to the story of Joseph and Potiphar, put the following sign on the board in bold letters:

   MAN JAILED DUE TO WOMAN'S LIE!

5. As an introduction to the story of Jacob and Rachel, hand each student an index card with the following instructions on it:

   Write down something for which you would work for seven years. For fourteen years.

6. Hand out a sheet with a game that will get them quickly involved in the lesson. For example:

   Which of these names are in *Megillat Esther*? (The letters are in the wrong order.)

   1. AAHMN (Haman)
   2. USDHJ (Judah)
   3. RDOMCAEI (Mordecai)
   4. SOSEM (Moses)
   5. RHSETE (Esther)
   6. OMINA (Naomi)
   7. SRHOESHUHAIVS (Ahashveirosh)

   Can you name this person? (There are letters missing in each name.)

   1. M__ __ __ __ (Moses)
   2. D__ __ __ __ BEN __ __ __ __ ON (David Ben Gurion)
   3. Q__ __ __N E__ __H __ __ (Queen Esther)
   4. A__ __ E F__ __ __K (Anne Frank)

15. Inquiring Minds Want to Know

Overview

This simple technique stimulates the curiosity of students by encouraging speculation about a topic or question. Students are more likely to retain knowledge about previously uncovered subject matter if they are involved from the onset in a full class learning experience.

Procedure

1. Ask an intriguing question of the class in order to stimulate curiosity about a subject you want to discuss. The question posed should be one to which you expect that no student knows the answer.

   There are many categories of such questions. Here are a few examples:

   - *Everyday knowledge* (Why are fish considered *pareve*, not meat?)
   - *How to* (How do you make a *shofar*?)
   - *Definitions* (What does *teshuva* mean?)
   - *Titles* (What is the book of Numbers about?)
   - *The way things work* (How do you find the weekly portion in a *Torah* scroll?)
   - *Outcome* (How do you think this story will end?)

2. Encourage speculation and wild guessing. Use phrases such as "Take a guess" or "Take a stab at it."
3. Do not give feedback immediately. Accept all guesses. Build curiosity about the real answer.

4. Use the question as a lead-in to what you are about to teach. Include the answer to your question in your lesson. You should find that students are more attentive than usual.

Variations

1. Pair up students and ask them to collectively make a guess.
2. Instead of a question, tell students what you are about to teach them and why they should find it interesting. Try to spice up this introduction in somewhat the same fashion as "coming attractions" promote a movie.

Examples

Here are a variety of questions that might make your students curious.

- Did some Jews always live in Israel? (yes)
- Are Jews allowed to make up their own prayers? (yes)
- What is the REAL reason *H̲anukkah* is celebrated for eight days? (The Maccabees missed celebrating *Sukkot* and did so when they were finally victorious.)
- On what are the laws for Shabbat based? (the actions taken to build the *mishkan*)
- Before World War II, why did many Jews not leave Europe? (They had family and property there; they could not conceive of the horror that was to come.)
- Are there rules about how to build a synagogue? (no)
- How many Torah verses (*p'sukim)* does it take to tell the entire story of the Tower of Babel? (nine)
- Why was Sarah's tent open on all four sides? (as a symbol of her hospitality)
- Why did God create Shabbat last? (rest after creating the world)
- What does the *Mi Khamocha* prayer have to do with H̲anukkah? (The first letter of each word of the prayer spells *Maccabee*.)
- How can the use of scapegoat be a good thing in the Torah and bad thing today? What is the difference between the two usages? (The Torah scapegoat freed us from guilt; today a scapegoat is someone who takes the blame for something.)

- According to the Talmud, who should be fed first, an animal or its owner? (animal)
- If God knows everything, why did God need to ask Cain, "Where is your brother Abel?" (to draw his attention to what he had done)

16. Listening Teams

Overview

This activity is a way to help students stay focused and alert during a lesson. It works equally well for viewing films. Listening teams are small groups that are responsible for clarifying the class material covered in the lesson or film.

Procedure

1. Divide the students into four teams and give the teams these assignments:

Team	Role	Assignment
1	*Questioners*:	After the lesson/film, ask at least two questions about the material covered.
2	*Supporters*:	After the lesson/film, select points they agree with (or found helpful) and explain why.
3	*Critics:*	After the lesson/film, comment on anything you disagreed with (or found unhelpful) and explain why.
4	*Idea Givers:*	After the lesson/film, give specific ideas about or applications of the material.

2. Present the lesson/film. After it is over, give teams a few moments to complete their assignments.
3. Call on each team to question, agree, and so forth. You should obtain more student participation than you ever imagined.

Variations

1. Create other roles. For example, ask a team to summarize the lesson/film or ask a team to create questions that test students' understanding of the material.
2. Give out questions in advance that will be answered in the lesson/film. Challenge students to listen for the answers. The team that can answer the most questions wins.

Examples

1. Explain about the laws of *kashrut* and the reasons why many Jews keep kosher. After the lesson is over, have the questioners begin by asking questions about what you have presented. Next, ask the supporters to share why they think keeping kosher is a good practice. Let the critics follow with their comments. Finally, request that the idea-givers present suggestions for how to make keeping kosher less difficult than some believe it to be.
2. Show the movie *The Chosen*. After the movie is over, have the questioners begin by asking questions about anything in the movie they didn't understand. Next, ask the supporters to share what they liked about the movie. Let the critics follow with comments about anything they disliked about the film. Finally, request that the idea-givers present things all Jews could learn from the movie.
3. Read the story of the death of Aaron's sons, Nadab and Abihu (*Parshat Shemini).* Have the questioners ask any questions about the story they did not understand. Next, ask the supporters to defend God's punishment. Then ask the critics for objections to God's decision. Finally, have the idea-givers discuss how this story applies (doesn't apply) to worship today.

17. Analogies and Metaphors

Overview

The goal of this technique is to create a comparison between the teacher's material and the knowledge and experience that the students already have.

Procedure

1. Decide on a concept you would like to teach that might be difficult for your students to understand. Or you may simply want to make points that will not easily be forgotten.
2. Think of a comparison to something familiar to your students that might serve as a bridge for understanding. It might be:
   - A familiar object (a tree of knowledge)
   - A popular expression ("Give me one more chance")
   - A common experience (getting up in the morning)
   - A physical activity (making a sand castle)
   - A well-known person (Martin Luther King)
   - A song title ("The Wheels on the Bus")
   - An animal (a snake)
3. Make the comparison to the concept you want to teach. For example, explain the *Neila* service on Yom Kippur with the phrase "Give me one more chance."

Variation

Ask students to come up with an analogy or metaphor of their own.

Examples

1. You are teaching Rosh ha-Shanah and present the following text. These are the words of a girl named Ilona that describe when she feels close to God.

   When you go on a plane, you are nearer to God because you can see the world, a lot of it, more than when you are on land, and you can realize how big the whole universe is, and people, they're not even visible. The cars are moving, and you know that people are there driving, but you can't see them. That's why you have to stop yourself (once in a while, at least) and say, "Are you remembering God, and are you looking at the big picture, the way He does, or are you inside a car, and all you're thinking of is where you want to go right away (and watch out, anyone else!)?"[5]

   This girl's description of being in an airplane can help the students discuss how we are to take stock of our lives on *Rosh ha-Shanah* (i.e., the concept of *ḫesbon ha nefesh*).

2. Provide a sentence stem for the students to complete, such as "God is like a rock because..." to begin a discussion of God's attributes. You can continue with other metaphors, such as "God is like a tree because..."

3. Have the class discuss how the *Shema* is like the Pledge of Allegiance to the flag (and how it is not).

[5] From Tiku Shofar. p. 86. Used with permission of Robert Coles, The Spiritual Life of Children. New York: Houghton Mifflin, 1990.

18. Acting It Out

SECTION 3. HOW TO HELP STUDENTS ACQUIRE KNOWLEDGE, SKILLS, AND ATTITUDES ACTIVELY

Overview

Sometimes, no matter how clear a verbal or visual explanation is, some things you want to teach don't sink in. One way to help develop a picture of the material is to ask some students to act out the concepts or walk through the procedures you are trying to get across.

Procedure

1. Choose a concept (or a set of related concepts) or a procedure that can be illustrated by acting it out. Examples include:
   - a verse in the *siddur* or in the Torah
   - finding the *shoresh* (root) of a Hebrew word
   - shaking a *lulav*
   - a Bible story
2. Use any of the following methods:
   - Have some students come to the front of the room and ask them to physically simulate aspects of the concept or procedure.
   - Create large cards that name the parts of a procedure or concept. Give out cards to some students. Place students with cards in such a way that they are correctly sequenced.
   - Develop a role-play in which students dramatize the material you are teaching. (Use puppets in primary grades.)
   - Using volunteer students, walk through a step-by-step procedure.
3. Discuss the learning drama that you have created. Make whatever teaching points you want.

Variations

1. Videotape a group of students illustrating the concept or procedure and show the tape to the class.
2. Ask students to create a way to act out a concept or procedure without your guidance.

Examples

1. For younger students, make puppets of characters in a Bible story and have them act out the story as a puppet show. Stories to consider include:
   - Adam and Eve in the Garden of Eden
   - Noah and his family building the ark and loading the animals.
   - Abraham and Sarah providing hospitality to the angels (dressed as strangers)
   - Joseph and his brothers (any part of the story)
   - Moses and Aaron meeting with Pharaoh
   - Miriam's dance and the Israelites' crossing of the Red Sea
   - A scene from *Megillat Esther*
   - Rebecca at the well
2. For any age, read the *brakhot* in *Birkhot ha-Shahar* that express our daily gratitude to God. (Be sure to simplify the language when needed.) As you read each *brakhah*, invite your students to do a physical movement that captures its meaning. For instance, "who crowns the people Israel with glory" can be accompanied by a movement suggesting a crown being placed on someone's head. If you think that this activity would be too difficult for your students, do a movement yourself and have students imitate you. They will soon get the idea and be able to initiate a movement.
3. Use sign language to depict a prayer. You may use American Sign Language or ask students to give you a hand motion for each word (e.g., the words of the *Shema* or the words listing the order of the Passover *seder*).
4. Ask younger students to pretend they are a Jewish symbol such as a candle or *kiddush* cup. They can pantomime how they look as well as what they do.

19. Meet the Press

Overview

This activity is an excellent way to involve students and guest speakers in an engaging learning experience. It gives students the opportunity to take an active role in preparing for the guest speaker so they will be more attentive and eager to participate.

Procedure

1. Invite a guest speaker(s) to address your class on the subject you are currently studying, such as the Holocaust, Israel, the Jewish community, Jews around the world.
2. Prepare the guest speaker by telling him or her that the session will be conducted like a press conference. In keeping with that format, the speaker is to prepare a few brief remarks or an opening statement and then be prepared to answer questions from the press.
3. Prior to the guest's appearance, prepare the students by discussing how a press conference is conducted and then giving them an opportunity to formulate several questions to ask the speaker.
4. As an alternative to a live guest, dress up as a person (living or dead) whom students can interview.

Variations

1. You may choose to have several guests at the same time and conduct roundtable discussions. Seat each guest at a table or in a circle of chairs to share information and experiences with a small group. The group members will have an opportunity to interact with the

guest by asking questions in a more personal environment. Divide the class session into a series of rounds. Determine the length of each round, depending on the time available and the number of guests. In general, ten or fifteen minutes for each round is appropriate. Direct each small group to move from one guest to the next as the rounds progress. Shorten the time for younger students.

2. Invite some students from a previous class you taught to serve as visiting guest experts.
3. To teach younger students to do this activity, have some questions ready in a bag that they can pick out and ask. Then have them add their own questions. Questions could be divided into categories to ensure that all areas to be learned are covered.

Examples

1. A guest comes to class dressed as a *shtetl* character. The press asks the following questions (rotating each category):

   Home and Family
   - Did you live in a place where mostly Jews lived?
   - What was your house like?
   - Who else was in your family?
   - How did you celebrate Jewish holidays at your house?
   - What did you do in your free time?

   Work
   - What kind of work did you do?
   - Were you rich, poor, or in the middle?
   - Was there any work you were not allowed to do?
   - Did anyone else in your family work?
   - Who was in charge of the kitchen?

   Synagogue Life
   - What kind of synagogue did you have?
   - What did the rabbi do?
   - Was there a cantor?
   - Where could you buy Jewish books or ritual objects?
   - Did everyone in your neighborhood have the same ideas about being Jewish?

Learning

- Did you go to school?
- What did you study?
- What was your teacher like?
- What language did they use at school?
- Did you study as an adult?

2. Tell students that you are pretending to be God. Give the press these questions about why God created a flood over all the earth or invite them to create their own questions.
   - Were the people so bad that you had to do this?
   - Why did you decide to save Noah and his family?
   - Why did you include the animals in the ark?
   - Were you sorry you made the flood?
   - When we see a rainbow, can we really believe you won't destroy the world again?
3. Tell students that you are pretending to be Esau. Have them interview Esau. The following are questions they might ask.
   - Were you really hungry when you traded your birthright for lentil soup?
   - Did you care about the birthright at all?
   - Were you angrier at your mother or your brother when they fooled Isaac?
   - Why did you eventually forgive Jacob?
   - Were you happy or relieved that you two did not live in the same place as adults?
4. Have four students pretend to be the four matriarchs. The following are questions their classmates might ask.
   - Do you think your story was fully told in the Torah?
   - What else do you think should have been included?
   - How did you feel about your husbands? Your children?
   - How do you feel about your recent inclusion in the *Amidah* in many prayer books?

Class Discussion

All too often a teacher tries to stimulate class discussion but is met with uncomfortable silence as students wonder who will dare to speak up first. Starting a discussion is no different from beginning a lesson. You have to build interest first! The strategies that follow are sure-fire ways to stimulate discussion. Some will even create heated but manageable exchanges between students. All of them are designed so that *every* student is involved.

20. Active Debate

Overview

A debate can be a valuable method of promoting thinking and reflection, especially if students are expected to take a position contrary to their own. This is a strategy for a debate that actively involves every student in the class, not just the debaters.

Procedure

1. Develop a statement that takes a position on a controversial issue relating to your subject matter (e.g., "The Jewish people should not be divided into separate movements because it creates too much disunity").
2. Divide the class into two debating teams. Assign (arbitrarily) the pro position to one group and the con position to the other.
3. Next, create two to four subgroups within each debating team. In a class of twenty-four students, for example, you might create three pro subgroups and three con subgroups, each containing four members. Ask each subgroup to develop arguments for its assigned position. (Or provide an extensive list of arguments they might discuss and select from.) At the end of their discussion, have the subgroup select a spokesperson.
4. Set up two to four chairs (depending on the number of subgroups created for each side) for the spokespersons of the pro side, and facing them, the same number of chairs for the spokespersons of the con side. Place the remaining students behind their debate team. For the example above, the arrangement will look like this:

```
x                 x
x                 x
x   pro   con     x
x   pro   con     x
x   pro   con     x
x                 x
x                 x
```

Begin the debate by having the spokespersons present their views. Refer to this process as "opening arguments."

5. After everyone has heard the opening arguments, stop the debate and reconvene the original subgroups. Ask the subgroups to strategize how to counter the opening arguments of the opposing side. Again, have each subgroup select a spokesperson, preferably a new person.
6. Resume the debate. Have the spokespersons, seated across from each other, give counter-arguments. As the debate continues (be sure to alternate between sides) encourage other students to pass notes to their debaters with suggested arguments or rebuttals. Urge them to cheer or applaud the arguments of their debate team representatives.
7. When you think it appropriate, end the debate. Instead of declaring a winner, reconvene the entire class in a single circle. Be sure to integrate the class by having students sit next to people who were on opposite sides. Hold a class-wide discussion on what students learned about the issue from the debate experience. Ask students to identify what they thought were the best arguments raised on both sides.

Variations

1. Add one or more empty chairs to the debate teams. Allow students to occupy these empty chairs whenever they want to join the debate.

2. Start the activity immediately with the opening arguments of the debate. Proceed with a conventional debate, but frequently rotate the debaters.
3. With a small class (or younger students), have them begin in pairs, one being *aleph* and the other *bet*. The *alephs* are assigned the pro position and the *bets* the con position. They debate for a few minutes, and then the teacher surprises them by asking them to reverse their positions and continue debating. After this second round, if there are sufficient numbers, have each pair join with another pair to repeat the debate, including the reversal of positions. This reinforces the learning and gives confidence to more reticent students.

Examples

1. The debate topic: The prayer *Barukh shem k'vod malkhuto l'olam va'ed* (Blessed is the Name of Your glorious reign forever and ever) should always be said out loud, not just on Yom Kippur (or should only be said out loud on Yom Kippur).

   One side may point out that this verse was originally recited on Yom Kippur in the Holy of Holies and that we are preserving that tradition. Another argument might be that we should not forget that there were times in our history when saying that God, not the current king or emperor, ruled was dangerous. When the people gathered on Yom Kippur, they found the courage to shout out the verse. Therefore, reciting it out loud should be reserved for Yom Kippur.

   The other side may stress that since we live in a country where we are free to worship God in our own way, we should always say this verse out loud. It reinforces our beliefs in God and in democracy. Another point might be that elected officials come and go, but the rule of God is eternal. Hearing this verse teaches us to take politics seriously in order to create a society that reflects our values.

2. The debate topic: The *Shema* should always be said while standing (or sitting).

   One side may focus on how we give honor to the *Shema* and what it teaches us by standing. We stand for the *Amidah* and rise for the Torah. The *Shema* is from the Torah. Therefore, we should stand for the *Shema*. When we say the *Shema*, we are witnesses for God. Witnesses in court always rise.

The other side may focus on the concept of *kavannah* (intent). When we recite the *Shema*, we are proclaiming the oneness of God, which is the basis and foundation of our religion. The *Shema* says *listen*. We need to concentrate. When we are sitting, we are more comfortable. We are less distracted so we can really listen to the words and think about what they mean.

3. A prominent businessman offers to build a needed addition to a synagogue religious school. The community accepts the offer with gratitude. Soon after, he is found guilty of several unethical business practices in one of his stores. The businessman is fined and has to make restitution to certain clients. In an interview in a local newspaper he declares that he will not repeat this mistake and promises that he will never do this again.

   One side may argue that since those who were wronged were repaid what was owed to them, the funds for the school will not come from tainted money. Also, since he has done *teshuvah*, we should consider the slate clean and accept his gift.

   The other side may express the view that this money could be tainted. We cannot know for certain. Perhaps he cheated before but did not get caught. Anyhow, even if it is clean, the Jewish community should not be associated with this money or the person giving it.

21. Point–Counterpoint

Overview

This activity is an excellent technique to stimulate discussion and gain a deeper understanding of complex issues. The format is similar to a debate but is less formal and moves more quickly.

Procedure

1. Select an issue that has two or more sides.
2. Divide the class into groups according to the number of positions you have stated and ask each group to come up with arguments to support their side. Encourage them to work with seat partners or small cluster groups.
3. Reconvene the entire class, but ask members of each group to sit together with space between the small groups.
4. Explain that any student can begin the debate. After the student has had an opportunity to present one argument in favor of his or her assigned position, allow a different argument or counter-argument from other groups. Continue the discussion, moving quickly back and forth between or among the groups.
5. Conclude the activity by comparing the issues as you, the teacher, see them. Allow for follow-up reaction and discussion.

Variations

1. Instead of a group-on-group debate, pair individual students from different groups and have them argue with each other. This can be done simultaneously, so that every student is engaged in the debate at the same time.

2. Line up the opposing groups so that they are facing each other. As one person concludes his or argument, have that student toss an object (such as a ball or a beanbag) to a member of the opposing side. The person catching the object must rebut the previous person's argument.

Examples

Pro or con...

1. Shabbat is a spiritual experience only when observed strictly according to *halakhah*.
2. All Jews should make *aliyah* to Israel.
3. Holidays like Passover should be celebrated when families can actually get together, not necessarily on the Hebrew calendar date.
4. When there are only nine people, the Torah should be considered the tenth person to make a *minyan* (a quorum).
5. Abraham was more important to the Jewish people than Moses.
6. Now that our calendars are more precise, there is no need to have a second day of *yontif* (festival observance).
7. The words in *Hatikvah* should be changed from *nefesh yehudi* to *nefesh yisraeli* to be more inclusive of Israel's Christian and Muslim citizens.
8. After Jacob's death, Joseph's brothers told him a lie: "BEFORE HIS DEATH, YOUR FATHER LEFT THE FOLLOWING MESSAGE....SAY TO JOSEPH, 'FORGIVE I URGE YOU THE OFFENSE AND GUILT OF YOUR BOTHERS WHO TREATED YOU SO HARSHLY. THEREFORE, PLEASE FORGIVE THE OFFENSE OF THE SERVANTS OF THE GOD OF YOUR FATHERS'" (Genesis 50:15–17). This lie was wrong.
9. Noah did not do enough to warn his neighbors about the impending flood.
10. If we had wiped out Amalek, Jewish suffering would have been eliminated.

22. Three-Stage Fishbowl

Overview: A fishbowl is a discussion format in which a portion of the class forms a discussion circle and the remaining students form a listening circle around the discussion group (see "Methods to Get Participation at Any Time," p. 19). Below is one of the more interesting ways to set up a fishbowl discussion.

Procedure

1. Devise three questions for discussion relevant to your subject matter. In a class on Passover, for example, the questions might be:
   - Why do we ask the same four questions at the seder each year?
   - Why were all the Egyptians punished, not just Pharaoh?
   - Just as our ancestors left for freedom in haste, we must move quickly to work for freedom and justice. What requires our immediate attention?

   Ideally, the questions should be interrelated. Decide in what order you would like the questions discussed.
2. Set up chairs in a fishbowl configuration (two concentric circles). Have the students count off by 1, 2, and 3. Ask the members of Group 1 to occupy the discussion-circle seats and ask the members of groups 2 and 3 to sit in the outer-circle seats. Pose your first question for discussion. Allow up to ten minutes for discussion (less for younger students). Invite one student to facilitate the discussion or act as the facilitator yourself.
3. Next, invite the members of Group 2 to sit in the inner circle, replacing Group 1 members, who now sit in the outer circle. Ask the members of Group 2 if they would like to make any brief comments about the first discussion and then segue into the second discussion topic.

4. Follow the same procedure with members of the third discussion group.

5. When all three questions have been discussed, reconvene the class as one discussion group. Ask them for their reflections on the entire discussion.

Variations

1. If it is not possible to have circles of chairs, have a rotating panel discussion instead. One third of the class becomes panelists for each discussion question. The panelists can sit in front of the classroom facing the remainder of the class.

2. For younger students, use only one discussion question rather than three. Invite each subsequent group to respond to the discussion of the preceding group.

Examples

The Purim Megillah

1. What were the personality traits of Vashti? Esther? Ahashveirosh? Mordecai? Haman?

2. What do you think life was like for Esther in the king's palace?

3. How did you feel about the rewards that Esther and Mordecai received at the end of the *Megillah*? Did either get a better deal?

The Four Children from the *Haggadah*

1. Do you think the response to the *wise child* is enough?

2. Why do you think the response to the *wicked child* is so harsh?

3. The *tam* is usually translated as "simple" but can also be translated as "whole" or "perfect". Which translation do you think is better?

The Lower East Side circa 1900

1. How was the new land different for the rich and the poor?

2. How did the people shop?

3. Why did parents work so hard?

23. Trial by Jury

Overview

This technique utilizes a mock trial complete with witnesses, prosecutors, defenders, friends of the court, and more. It is a good method to spark controversy learning—learning by effectively arguing a viewpoint and challenging the opposite view.

Procedure

1. Create an indictment that will help students see different sides of an issue. For example, *indict Jacob for favoring one of his sons, indict God for the devastation of the flood, indict Rebecca and Jacob for tricking Isaac.*
2. Assign roles to students. Depending on the number of students, you could use all or some of these roles: *defendant, defense attorney, defense witnesses, prosecuting attorney, prosecution witnesses, friends of the court, judge, jury member.* Each role can be filled by one person or by a team. You could have any number in the jury.
3. Allow time for students to prepare. This could be a few minutes or up to an hour, depending on the complexity of the issue. Note that students do not have to do all of the preparation at one session. This activity can be combined with other class work. However, they should work on this assignment at consecutive sessions so they do not lose momentum.
4. Conduct the trial. Consider using these activities: *opening arguments, case presented by the prosecutor and witnesses, friend-of-the-court briefs, closing arguments, etc.*

5. Conduct the jury deliberations. These should be done publicly, so everyone can hear how the evidence is being weighed. Non-jury members can be given an assignment to listen for various aspects of the case.

Variations

1. Extend the activity by staging a retrial.
2. Eliminate a trial by jury and substitute a trial by judge only.
3. Invite another class to serve as the jury.

Example

1. A trial could be set up to indict Abraham for his willingness to sacrifice Isaac.

   The prosecuting attorney can accuse Abraham of not arguing with God about this order, unlike what he did with Sodom and Gomorrah. Sarah can serve as a prosecution witness, stating how Abraham left to sacrifice Isaac without even telling her. The angel can testify that Abraham did, in fact, bind Isaac. The defense attorney can present the case that Abraham was compelled to act by the command of a higher power. Abraham's servants may testify for the defense that Abraham told them that they (he and Isaac) would be returning, so there was no plan to actually kill Isaac. This was Abraham's way of testing God, to see if God really wanted this outcome (Isaac's sacrifice).

2. A trial could be set up to indict God for the overzealous punishment of the ten spies (*Parshat Shelah Lekha*).

   The prosecuting attorney can accuse God of punishing ten of the spies for giving an accurate report about the Promised Land. Israelites from their tribes can be witnesses who claim that the ten brought back a branch with a heavy cluster of grapes, indicating the bountiful nature of the land, and also claimed that the inhabitants were large and powerful, like giants. Their report seemed balanced. For the defense, Moses could testify that their report instilled fear and prevented the people from conquering the land. The defense attorney could explain how a report that viewed the situation from a negative perspective demoralized the people and was grounds for treason.

Cooperative Learning

One of the best ways to promote active learning is to give learning assignments that are carried out in small groups of students. The peer support and diversity of viewpoints, knowledge, and skill help make collaborative learning a valuable part of your classroom learning climate. However, cooperative learning is not always effective. There may be unequal participation, poor communication, and confusion instead of real learning. The strategies that follow are designed to maximize the benefits of cooperative learning and to minimize the pitfalls.

24. Card Sort

Overview

This is a collaborative activity that can be used to teach concepts, teach classification characteristics, teach facts about objects, or review information. The physical movement featured can help to energize a tired class.

Procedure

1. Give each student an index card that contains information that fits into one or more categories. Here are some examples:
   - things associated with different holidays
   - characters in various books of the Bible
   - prayers about petition, praise, or gratitude
   - Hebrew words or different parts of speech (nouns, verbs, adjectives)
2. Ask students to mill around the room and find others whose cards fit the same category. (You may announce the categories beforehand or let them be discovered by the students.)
3. Have students with cards in the same category present themselves to the rest of the class.
4. As each category is presented, make any teaching points you think are important.

Variations

1. Ask each group to make a lesson about its category.
2. At the beginning of the activity, form teams. Give each team a complete set of cards. Be sure they are shuffled so that the cat-

egories into which students are to be sorted are not obvious. Ask each team to sort the cards into categories. Each team can obtain a score for the number of cards sorted correctly.

Examples

1. If you are teaching *brakhot* for eating food, create cards (with either pictures or words) for each *brakhah*—apples and oranges for *borei pri ha-etz,* potato and carrots for *borei pri ha-adamah,* bread and onion roll for *hamozti lehem min ha-aretz*, pretzels and cake for *borei minei mezonot*, milk and meat for *sh'hakol n'heyeh b'dvaro*. Mix the cards. Have students sort them by *brakhah*.
2. Students are given various *brakhot* and must sort them according to whether the *brakhot* are recited upon *seeing, smelling* or *tasting* something.
3. Younger students can be given a few simple items to sort by holiday, such as pictures of a menorah, dreidles and latkes (Hanukkah) or pictures of a *megillah*, costumes, and *hamentashen* (Purim).
4. Sarah, Rebecca, Rachel, and Leah are in the Genesis category, while Moses, Miriam, and Aaron appear in Exodus.
5. Hebrew words that begin with *alef* or with *ayin* are sorted correctly.
6. After a unit on Jewish theology, give high school students a pack of cards with names of theologians and another pack that contains key words based on their ideas. Have students match theologians with their main ideas (e.g., Martin Buber with "I and Thou," Mordecai Kaplan with " Judaism as a Civilization").

25. Learning Tournament

Overview

This technique combines small-group study and team competition and can be used to promote the learning of a wide variety of facts, concepts, and skills.

Procedure

1. Divide students into teams with two to eight members. Make sure the teams have equal numbers. (If this cannot be achieved, you will have to average each team's score.)
2. Provide them with material to study together.
3. Develop several questions that test comprehension and/or recall of the learning material. Use formats that make self-scoring easy, such as multiple choice, fill in the blank, true/false, or terms to define.
4. Give a portion of the questions to students. Refer to this as round one of the learning tournament. **Each student must answer the questions individually.**
5. After the questions have been given, provide the answers and ask students to count the number they answered correctly. Then have them pool their scores with every other member of their team to obtain a team score. Announce the scores of each team.
6. Ask the team to study again for the second round of the tournament. Then ask more test questions as part of round two. Have teams once again pool their scores and add them to their round-one score.

7. You can have as many rounds as you would like, but **be sure to allow the team to have a study session between each one**. (The length of a learning tournament can also vary. For most classes, a few rounds works well.)

Variations

1. Penalize students for wrong answers by assigning them a score of -2 or -3. If they are unsure of the answer, a blank answer can be counted as 0.
2. Make the performance of a series of skills the basis of the tournament.

Examples

1. Use prayer vocabulary words or phrases that you would like students to learn or review. Give approximately six words per round for students to learn in teams (for example, *barukh atah eloheinu, gadol, gibor, h̲asadim tovim*). Each round could focus on a different prayer. At the end of the activity, test the class to assess achievement.
2. Have students in teams learn facts about the State of Israel. Round one could focus on the three major cities in Israel—Jerusalem, Haifa, and Tel Aviv. Round two could feature information on the location of Israel's neighbors—Lebanon, Syria, Jordan, and Egypt. Round three could have pictures and explanations of symbols one might see in Israel (menorah, Hamsa, and Magen David). Then,conduct the tournament.
3. Teach each of the seder's traditional Four Questions in a separate round. You may focus on the vocabulary as well as the recitation. Give teams a chance to practice. Then create a competition in which students must recite the questions correctly. At the conclusion of the activity, have the class sing them all together.

26. The Power of *Hevruta*

Overview

This activity is used to promote cooperative learning and reinforce the importance and benefits of synergy—that is, that two heads are better than one. In Jewish learning, a group of two is called a *hevruta*.

Procedure

1. Give students one or more questions that require reflection. Here are some examples about God:
   - What difference does it make that God is One?
   - Why does God allow bad things to happen to good people?
2. Ask students to answer the questions individually.
3. After all students have completed their answers, arrange students into pairs and ask them to share their answers with each other.
4. Ask the pairs to create a new answer to each question, improving on each individual's response.
5. When all pairs have written new answers, compare the answers of each pair to others in the class.

Variations

1. Invite the entire class to select the best answer for each question.
2. To save time, assign specific pairs specific questions rather than having all pairs answer all questions.

Examples

1. Ask the question "What does the shofar teach us?"

   One student may write that it announces a new year. Another may write that it tells us to wake up and behave better. They may combine their answers to say the shofar teaches us that we can act better in the new year.

2. Ask the question: "What difference does it make that there is a State of Israel?"

   One student may write that it makes all Jews feel safe. Another student may write that it's the one place where Jewish celebrations can happen more fully and people speak Hebrew. They may combine their answers to say Israel provides a safe homeland for all Jews. There Jews can more fully celebrate Jewish holidays and speak Hebrew.

3. Ask the question: "Why did God choose Abraham to be the father of the Jewish people?"

   One student may write that Abraham believed in one God. Another student may write that he was a good person who could think for himself. They may combine their answers to say Abraham was a good person who thought of the idea of one God.

4. Ask students to interpret the Zionist slogan "If you will it, it is no legend."

   One student may write that if you really want something, you can make it happen. Another student may write that your thoughts may start an action. Together they may write "If you have an idea and feel strongly about it, you can put your thoughts into action and make it happen."

5. Ask the question "Why might the cloning of a human being be a problem?"

   One student may write that cloning may cause inbreeding, thereby reducing human survival. Another student may write that cloning will create fewer individual differences in people (preferred characteristics). Their combined answer might be that less variation in humans could reduce human survival and make people lose respect for individual differences.

27. Small-Group Study

Overview

This method gives students the responsibility to learn together. Each will benefit from the expertise and support of the other members of their group.

Procedure

1. Divide your class into small groups of three or four students.
2. Make sure each has a separate space in which to work.
3. Give students material to study or assign them a particular task. Directions for this should be clear and simple.
4. Assign roles—e.g., leader, note-taker, time-keeper, presenter.
5. After the assignment, reconvene the entire group and do one of the following:
   - A "*presenter*" from each group shares what each group learned. (This does not necessarily mean all that was learned. Each group, for example, could share the answer to one question.)
   - Quiz students.
   - Review the material together.
   - Ask students to rate how well they now know the material.

Variations

1. At the end of the activity, have two study groups combine to share notes on what they have learned.
2. Younger students can use drawings, pictures, or charts to show their knowledge.

Examples

1. Here is a small-group learning activity for younger students on Jewish symbols.[6]

   After visiting the synagogue to see Jewish symbols, put students into small groups to help one another recall important information about them.

   - Distribute a set of synagogue symbol cards to each group.
   - Explain that you will ask a series of questions about synagogue symbols, and they will need to decide together which word or picture card in the pack answers each question. The team should have the correct card ready to show the rest of the class.
   - Ask a question, such as "Where is the Torah kept?"
   - Have one member from each group hold up the answer card. (This responsibility can rotate.) You can do this with or without keeping score.

2. Here is a lesson on a Torah *parshah* for elementary students:
   - After studying a Torah *parsha* or section of a *parsha* (e.g., Joseph in Egypt), put students into small groups to create a five-minute skit about what they learned.
   - Students should first recall all of the relevant information. (The note-keeper records this.) Then they proceed to write their skits.
   - Reconvene the class and have each group present their skit.
   - Have students compare what each group chose to emphasize.

3. Here is a small-group learning activity on Jewish history for older students.
   - Divide the class into small groups.
   - Give each group a short handout with reading material. Give the students a limited time to read (by themselves or out loud).
   - Ask each group to list at least three reasons that Jews chose to emigrate to the United States at the turn of the century or the reasons Moses was not permitted to enter the land of Israel or the difference between the terms *kavannah* and *kevah*.
   - When time is up, ask each group to share one answer until all proposed answers are presented.

[6] From a workshop conducted by Sallie Olson on cooperative learning.

28. Group-to-Group Exchange

Overview

In this strategy, different assignments are given to different groups of students. Each group then teaches what it has learned to the rest of the class.

Procedure

1. Select a topic in which there are different ideas, events, positions, concepts, or approaches to assign. The topic should be one that promotes an exchange of views or information (as opposed to a debate). Here are some examples:
   - the position of the four movements (Orthodox, Conservative, Reform, and Reconstructionist) on *halakhah*
   - the key ideas of two or more Jewish theologians (e.g., Rav Kook and Franz Rosenzweig)
   - the different views of *H̲assidim* and *Mitnagdim* on prayer
2. Divide the class into groups corresponding to the number of assignments. In most cases, two to four groups are appropriate for this activity. Give each sufficient time to prepare how they could present the topic that has been assigned. For example, one group might present a summary of *parshat B'haalotekha,* and the second group might present a summary of *parshat Sh'lah̲ Lekha.*
3. When the preparation phase is completed, ask groups to select a spokesperson. Invite each spokesperson to address the other group(s).

4. After a brief presentation, encourage students to ask questions of the presenter or to offer their own views. Allow other members of the spokesperson's group to respond.
5. Continue the remaining presentations so that each group gives its information and has responded to audience questions and comments. Compare and contrast the views and information that were exchanged.

Variations

1. Ask groups to do extensive research before their presentations.
2. Use a panel format for each of the small-groups presentations. Have each presenter become a panelist. As the teacher, you can serve as moderator.

Examples

1. Students are asked to read the Tower of Babel story. Each small group is given a different question to answer, and groups present their responses to the rest of the class.
   - Why might the people who built the tower be afraid of being scattered over the world?
   - What is God's concern about the tower?
   - In today's world, is it a good or bad thing that people don't speak the same language?
2. Students are divided into three small groups, and each group is asked to study one of three prayers from the Rosh ha-Shanah liturgy—*Avinu Malkeinu, Zakhreinu L'Haim, Anu Amekha*—and then answer the following questions about their prayer:
   - What does this prayer say?
   - How do you feel about this prayer?
   - If a person took this prayer seriously, how might it affect his or her behavior?
3. Students are asked to read the story of Jacob wrestling with a *malakh* (messenger, angel, stranger). Each small group is asked to answer one of the following questions:
   - Why is Jacob troubled? (Think of as many reasons as possible.)

- Who is the stranger, and why do he and Jacob wrestle?
- Why does Jacob ask for a blessing, and what blessing does he receive?

Have students share what they learned using the technique described above.

29. Jigsaw Learning

Overview

Jigsaw learning is a widely practiced technique that is similar to group-to-group exchange, with one important difference: Every student presents or teaches something. It is an exciting alternative whenever there is material to be learned that can be segmented or "chunked" and where no one segment must be taught before the others. Each student learns something that, when combined with the material learned by others, forms a coherent body of knowledge or skill.

Procedure

1. Choose learning material that can be broken into parts. A segment can be as short as one sentence or as long as several pages. (If the material is lengthy, ask students to read their assignments before class.)

   Examples include:

   - prayers
   - holidays or different customs for a single holiday
   - famous Jewish personalities
   - Hebrew vocabulary words

2. Count the number of learning segments and the number of students. In an equitable manner, give out assignments to groups of students. For example, imagine a class of twelve students. Assume that you can divide learning materials into three segments or chunks. You might then be able to form quartets, assigning each group segment 1, 2, or 3. Then ask each quartet or study group to read, discuss, and learn the material assigned to them. (If you

wish, you can form two pairs or "study buddies" first and then combine the pairs into a quartet to consult and share with each other.) Younger students will find it easier to follow the jigsaw plan if you give each study group or buddy an index card of the same color. Then, when they form jigsaw groups, students will have different-color cards.

3. After the study period, form jigsaw learning groups. Such groups contain a representative of every study group in the class. In the example just given, the members of each quartet could count off 1, 2, 3, and 4. Then, form jigsaw learning groups of students with the same number. The result will be four trios. In each trio there will be one person who has studied segment 1, one for segment 2, and one for segment 3. The diagram below displays this sequence.

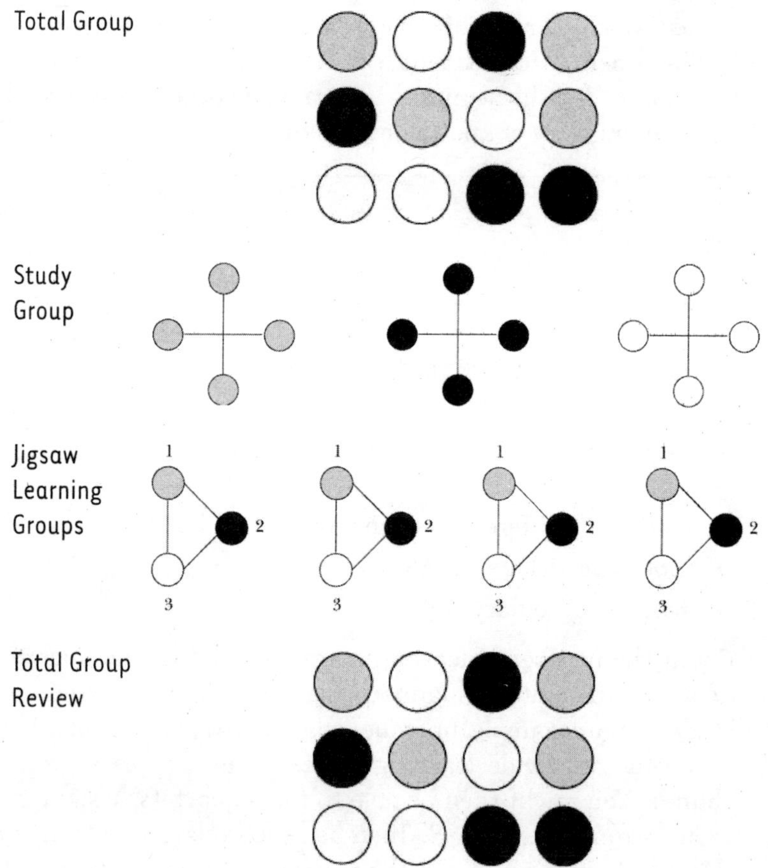

In many instances the number of students cannot be divided evenly into the number of learning segments. If this is the case, you can adjust by using learning partners instead of subgroups. Divide the learning material into only two segments, assigning one segment to one member of a pair and the other segment to his or her partner. For example, in a seven-part assignment, one person can be assigned parts 1–4, and the partner can be assigned parts 5–7. You can easily create study buddies with the same assignment. Then have the original pair teach each other what they have studied.

4. Ask the members of the jigsaw groups to teach each other what they have learned.
5. Reconvene the full class for review and remaining questions to ensure accurate understanding.

Variations

1. Give a new task, such as answering a group of questions, that depends on the accumulated knowledge of all the members of a jigsaw learning group.
2. Assign to different students the responsibility to learn a skill rather than cognitive information. Have students teach one another the skills they have learned.

Examples

1. For younger students, have study group A learn the blessing for the candles; group B, the blessing for the wine; and group C, the blessing for the *ḥallah*. Then they form a jigsaw to teach one another all three blessings.
2. The Joseph story is divided into three chronological segments. Each of the three groups will study one segment and then, in a jigsaw, each segment is taught.
3. Study group A learns texts about the first three commandments. Study group B learns about the middle three, and study group C learns about the final four. In jigsaw groups they learn all Ten Commandments.
4. Each study group learns five new vocabulary words. They teach their new words to other students in their jigsaw groups. Finally,

the jigsaw groups are given a paragraph to translate together that contains all the new vocabulary words. (Younger students can learn just one or two new words.)

5. To learn about early Zionist leaders, study group A is given information about Chaim Weizmann, study group B is given information about Rabbi Abraham Iaaac Kook, and study group C is given information about David Ben Gurion. The students share their knowledge with each other in jigsaw groups. At the next session, study groups are formed to learn about Henrietta Szold, Golda Meir, and Vladimir Jabotinsky. Again the learning is shared.

30. Poster Presentations

Overview

This method is an excellent way to teach each other. It is also a novel and graphic way of enabling students to express their perceptions and feelings about the topic you are currently discussing in a non-threatening environment.

Procedure

1. Ask every student to select a topic related to the general class topic or unit being discussed or studied.
2. Request that students prepare a visual display of their concept on poster board, bulletin board, etc. (You will determine the size.) The poster display should be self-explanatory, so that observers would easily understand the idea without any further written or oral explanation. However, students may choose to prepare a one-page handout to accompany the poster, offering more detail and serving as further reference material.
3. During the designated class session, ask students to post their visual lessons and freely circulate around the room, viewing and discussing one another's posters.

Variations

1. You may choose to form teams of two or three instead of having students work individually.
2. Follow up a poster session with a panel discussion, using some displayers as panelists.

3. If your students know how, have them design computer-generated presentation slides.
4. Photographs can be incorporated into a mural. For example, students may use photographs of themselves for a depiction of the idea that *we were all present at Sinai.*

Examples

Posters could display:

- Prayers that have a theme—e.g., *ahavah* (love) might include *ahavat olam, ahavah rabbah*, and *shalom rav.*
- *Shtetl* life
- Three stages of Jewish immigration to the United States (Sephardic, Germanic, and Eastern European)
- The observance of Jewish life-cycle events
- The lives of Abraham and Sarah
- The ten chapters of the *Megillah*
- *Birkot ha-Shaḇar* (the Morning Blessings)
- The story of the Exodus from Egypt
- The seven *Minim* (species indigenous to the land of Israel)
- The story of Creation
- The holiday symbols
- Mothers in the book of Genesis and/or Exodus
- Current-day Maccabees (have students select)
- Photos of students acting out something that shows how to live
- In God's image[7]
- The theme of deception in Jacob's life
- A collage of articles and photos that depict how the media sometimes shames people *(bushah)* unnecessarily.
- The theme of partnership with God in caring for the earth and helping its inhabitants

[7]Suggested by Rabbi Richie Fagan, Auerbach CAJE consultant to Traditional and Conservative School.

Affective Learning

Affective learning activities help students to examine their feelings, values, and attitudes. The strategies that follow are designed to bring into awareness the feelings, values, and attitudes that accompany many Jewish classroom topics. They gently push students into examining their beliefs and deepening their spirituality.

31. Imagine That...

Overview

Through visual imagery students can imagine an idea, a concept, or an action in their minds and have an experience that gives them insight and brings important emotions to the surface.

Procedure

1. Introduce the topic that will be covered. Explain to students that the subject requires creativity and that the use of visual imagery may assist their efforts.
2. Instruct the class to close their eyes. Introduce a relaxation exercise that will clear current thoughts from the students' minds. (Optional: Use background music or dimmed lights to achieve results.)
3. Conduct warm-up exercises to open the mind's eye. Ask students, with their eyes closed, to try to visualize sights and sounds such as a rosebud, their bedroom, a changing traffic light, or the patter of rain.
4. When class members are relaxed and warmed up, provide an image for them to build upon. Suggestions include:
   - an experience many years ago (e.g., the expulsion from Spain)
   - a difficult situation (e.g., hearing an anti–Semitic remark)
   - an activity (e.g., searching for *hometz*)
5. As the image is described, provide regular silent intervals so that students can build their own visual images. Build in questions that encourage the use of all senses, such as:
   - What does it look like?

- Whom do you see? What are they doing?
- What do they/you feel?

6. Finish guiding the image and instruct class members to remember their image. Slowly end the exercise.
7. Ask students to form small groups and to share their imagery experiences. Ask them to describe to one another the image, using as many senses as possible. Or ask them to write about it.

Variations

1. Forgo students closing their eyes if it leads to immature behavior. Visualization will work by merely saying "Imagine that".
2. Now that students have rehearsed in their minds how they would act in a specific situation, invite them to plan how they might actually act on their thoughts.

Examples

1. Have your students imagine any of the following scenes from the Torah and the feelings evoked:
   - Being in Noah's ark for forty days and nights
   - Joseph showing his brothers his coat of many colors
   - Seeing the burning bush
   - Being a slave in Egypt
   - Crossing the Red Sea
   - Standing at Sinai
   - Opening the door at your seder and finding Elijah standing there
2. Have your students imagine how they would handle the following situations:
   - Being told by a Christian friend that Christmas is better than Hanukkah
   - Helping a blind person for a day
   - Making mistakes at their bar or bat mitzvah ceremony
   - Forgetting that it is Passover and eating bread or other kinds of *chometz*

- Asking parents if your family could have a Friday night Shabbat dinner with rituals.

3. Have your students imagine that they have the following opportunities:
   - Being able to invite any guest to their Passover seder. Whom would they invite and why?
   - Being able to participate in an archeological dig. What would they want to discover?
   - Being the wealthiest person in town. How would they spend their money?
   - Being able to change one event in Jewish history. What would it be and why?

32. Sentence Stems

SECTION 3. HOW TO HELP STUDENTS ACQUIRE KNOWLEDGE, SKILLS, AND ATTITUDES ACTIVELY

Overview

This strategy prompts students to think about and express beliefs and opinions on important issues, experiences, and emotions.

Procedure

1. Have students sit in a circle.
2. Present sentence stems that gently push students to express themselves. Phrases you can use include:
   - I think...
   - I am like...
   - I like/dislike...
   - My favorite...
   - I am afraid when...
   - I am happy when...
   - I feel...
   - I wonder...
   - I wish...
3. Going around the circle, ask students to complete the sentences by themselves. Students should have the right to pass if they do not wish to respond.

Variations

1. You do not have to ask the entire class to respond to one sentence stem. You can change after three or four students.

2. Completed sentence stems could be shared with a partner or a small group.

Examples

Any of these sentence stems would encourage your students to share their innermost thoughts and feelings in a safe way:

1. I feel close to God when...
2. I am like God when I...
3. I wish that God would...
4. I am grateful that God...
5. I think God is great because...
6. My favorite Jewish holiday is...
7. My favorite character in the Purim *Megillah* is...
8. My favorite thing to do on Shabbat is...
9. I think Jews today should...
10. Something I like (or dislike) about being Jewish is...
11. When I hear about a terrorist bombing in Israel, I feel...
12. The most important thing that the Jewish people gave to the world is...
13. The world would be a better place if everyone ...
14. I wonder if Moses...
15. I am proud that I am Jewish when...
16. What Shabbat peace means to me is...
17. As Jews, being members of the covenant, our job is to...

33. • Seeing How It Is

Overview

Often a topic promotes understanding of and sensitivity to people or situations that are unfamiliar to students. One of the best ways to accomplish this goal is to create an affective activity that simulates what that unfamiliar person or situation is like.

Procedure

1. Choose a type of person or situation that you want students to learn about. Here are some examples:
   - what it's like to be slaves in Egypt
   - what it's like to be in a different time period in Jewish history
   - what it's like to be from a different Jewish culture
   - what it's like to be a person with special problems or challenges
2. Create a way to simulate that person or situation. Among the ways to do this are the following:
   - Have students dress in the attire of the person or situation. Or have them handle the equipment, props, accessories, or other belongings of that person or situation or engage in a typical activity of that person.
   - Place students in situations in which they are required to respond as the role or character they have been given.
   - Use an analogy to build a simulation. Create a scenario that students are familiar with that sheds light on the unfamiliar situation. For example, you might ask all students who are left-handed to portray people who are culturally different than the rest of the students.

- Impersonate an individual and ask the students to interview you and find out about your experiences, views, and feelings.

3. Ask students how the simulation felt. Discuss the experience of being in someone else's shoes. Invite students to identify the challenges that unfamiliar persons and situations present to them.

Variations

1. If possible, arrange for real encounters with the unfamiliar situation or person.
2. Conduct a mental imagery experience in which students visualize the person or situation with which they are unfamiliar.

Examples

1. Sensitize students to elderly people by giving them eyeglasses smeared with Vaseline, dried peas to put in each shoe, cotton for each ear, and latex gloves for both hands. Then ask them to take out a pencil and paper and write down their name, address, and telephone number and to take a walk outside the classroom, opening the door and finding their way around. This could serve as an introduction to a *tzedakah* lesson on helping the elderly.
2. Teach the well-known song "If I Were a Rich Man" from *Fiddler on the Roof*. Ask students to imagine they are Teyve and discuss his experience and wishes. On the board, have students make a list of all the things that Tevye wishes he could do, including his greatest wish (thus focusing them on the importance of prayer and study in his value system). Ask them to tell how his dreams are different from theirs and how they are similar.
3. Ask students to imagine that they were living at the turn of the twentieth century, experiencing pogroms in Eastern Europe. What would they do and why?
   - remain in Europe?
   - emigrate to Israel?
   - emigrate to the United States?
4. Ask students to imagine that they were a part of the Exodus from Egypt. As they approached the Red Sea, they saw Pharaoh's army approaching with horses and chariots. How would they feel? What

thoughts would they have? (This would also work as a diary or journal writing exercise.)

5. Ask students to imagine that they are God, who hears Aaron and Miriam complaining about Moses marrying a Cushite woman. Would they defend Moses? What would they say? Would they punish either or both siblings? Have them compare their responses with those in *Parshat B'haalotkha*.
6. Ask students to imagine that Moses did not die in the wilderness and that he lived to enter the land of Israel. How do they think this would have changed the end of the Torah?

34. Billboard Ranking

Overview

Many learning situations contain no right or wrong content. When values, opinions, ideas, and preferences exist about a topic you are teaching, this activity can be used to stimulate reflection and discussion.

Procedure

1. Divide the class into small groups of three to four students.
2. Give students a list of any of the following:
   - different values (e.g., *tzedakah, gemilut hasidim*, etc.)
   - different opinions (e.g., Women should wear *kippot* if they are called to the Torah, women should not wear a *tallit*, etc.)
   - actions (e.g., the best way to honor your parents is to do well in school, do chores they want you to do, etc.)
3. Give each small group a Post-it™ pad. Ask them to write each item on the list on a separate sheet.
4. Next ask the small groups to sort the sheets so that the Post-it™ of the value, opinion, and action they prefer is on top and the remaining are placed in order of decreasing preference.
5. Create a billboard on which small groups can display their preferences. (The Post-it™ notes can be attached to a blackboard, a flip chart, or a large piece of paper.)
6. Compare and contrast the rankings that are now visually displayed.

Variations

1. Attempt to achieve a class-wide consensus.

2. Ask students to interview members of groups whose rankings differ from theirs.

Examples

1. Give each small group a copy of the Ten Commandments. Ask them to rank them (or the first or last five) according to importance.
2. Distribute three verses from *Pirke Avot* to each group and ask them to rank the verses according to which ones they feel offer the best advice.
3. Give pictures of three Jewish holidays to groups of younger students. Ask them to rank the pictures to reflect their favorites. Primary students could simply select their favorite holiday (from the three presented) for the billboard.
4. Ask younger students to rank biblical characters according to how important they think they are.

35. What? So What? Now What?

Overview:

The value of any experiential learning activity is enhanced by asking students to reflect on the experience they just had and to explore its implications. This reflection period is often referred to as processing or debriefing. Some experiential teachers now use the term "harvesting." Here is a three-stage sequence for harvesting a rich learning experience.

Procedure

1. Take the class through an experience that is appropriate to the topic you are teaching. The experience might include any of the following:
   - a game or simulation exercise
   - a field trip
   - a film
   - an action learning project
   - a debate
   - a role-play
   - a mental imagery exercise
2. Ask students to share **what** happened to them during the experience.

- What did you do?
  - What did you observe? What did you think about?
  - What feelings did you have during the experience?

3. Next ask students to ask themselves "**so what?**"
   - What benefits did you get from the experience?
   - What did you learn? What did you relearn?

- What are the lessons of the activity?
- How does the experience (if it is a simulation or role-play) relate to the real world?

4. Finally, ask students to consider "**now what?**"
   - How do you want to do things differently in the future?
   - How can you extend the learning you had?
   - What steps can you take to apply what you have learned?

Variations

1. Limit the discussion to "**what?**" and "**so what?**"
2. Use these questions to stimulate journal writing.

Examples

1. You are teaching about the Holocaust. Do the well-known activity of granting certain privileges (e.g., snack) to those with blue eyes or those wearing certain colors to elicit frustration and protests.
2. Give students earplugs to demonstrate the experience of deafness to your class. Give them important information and have them feel the difficulties of being hard of hearing.
3. Show a moving film such as *The Diary of Anne Frank* to make the Holocaust more real for students.
4. Visit a local nursing home to both entertain and get to know the residents.
5. Take your class to a matzah bakery to learn how matzah is made, including the laws that pertain to this process.
6. Have students role play the story of the burning bush to explore what it means to be conscious of God's presence.
7. Lead a guided imagery on Standing at Sinai to explore what it means that we all were present there.
8. Take your students on a *shiva* call to experience this mitzvah.

Follow the experience with What... So What... Now What questions. For example, you might ask students the following after visiting a nursing home:

- What did you see there?

- How did you feel during the visit?
- What did you learn from the visit?
- What did you get out of the visit for yourself?
- Would you like to visit a nursing home again?
- Do you want to do something to help elderly people? What?

36. Wrestling with Text

SECTION 3. HOW TO HELP STUDENTS ACQUIRE KNOWLEDGE, SKILLS, AND ATTITUDES ACTIVELY

Overview

This technique encourages students to probe the meanings and/or conflicts within a text.

Procedure

1. Divide the students into small groups.
2. Provide each one with an interesting text (from the Torah, the *siddur*, etc.)
3. Give students one of the following assignments:
   * Decide whether they agree or disagree with the text.
   - Read several opinions about the text. Discuss the merits of each one and then decide which opinion comes closest to their own.
   - Ask the question "How many things can we learn from this text?"
   - Have them write the text in their own words.

Variations

1. Give the small groups the same or different texts.
2. Focus on one word or one word at a time instead of the complete text.

Examples

1. Have students compare prayers in which God is referred to as He and in which God is referred to in gender-neutral terms.
2. Have students compare the verse in the traditional *Aliyah* blessing (being "called up" to the Torah) "Who has chosen us from

among all peoples" with the Reconstuctionist substitute "Who has brought us closer through worship."

3. Have students free-associate each Hebrew word of the *Shema* to explore what the words mean to them. (e.g., *Shema*—pay attention, follow; *Yisrael*—a people, land, Jacob)
4. Have students decide if they agree or disagree with these verses from *Pirke Avot:*
   - *Be exceedingly humble.*
   - *Say little and do much.*
5. Have students rank the following verses from the Torah in order of their personal meaning:
   - *You shall love your neighbor as yourself.*
   - *Justice, justice shall you pursue.*
   - *You shall be holy because I the Lord Your God am holy.*
6. After reading a short text (e.g., the *Aleinu* prayer) have students identify a word that stands out for them. Next they can identify a phrase, and then finally a word.
7. After reading the verse from *Pirke Avot* (2:5) "Do not separate yourself from the community," students can reflect on whether the priestly vestments violated this principle by setting priests apart and whether clergy today should wear anything different than their congregants.

37. Guided Meditation

Overview

This technique is a way of directing students to focus on a prayer to make it personally relevant.

Procedure

1. Give students an opportunity to settle down and get comfortable. (Optional: Shut off the lights and/or pull down the shades.)
2. Ask students to close their eyes.
3. Read from a prepared script or memorize what you will say. Use a soft, soothing voice so that you do not distract their thoughts. Read slowly, with a three- to five- second pause at the ellipses (...). End by reciting, singing or chanting the prayer.
4. Use the following introduction:
   - close your eyes...
   - take a deep breath... and another...
   - breathe in... breathe out...
5. Repeat the phrases "breathe in..." and "breathe out..." throughout the meditation.

Variation

You can vary the length of a meditation, depending on the age of the children.

Examples

1. Picture the sun

   And imagine yourself basking in its light...taking in its brightness and warmth...

Feeling comfort and pleasure...
Breathe in... and breathe out... (repeat)
Imagine that you are surrounded by God's light...
By God's presence...
God's blessings...
Breathe in... and breathe out... (repeat)
Picture the vastness of the universe... and imagine it filled with God's light... light that blocks out all darkness...
light that drapes the heavens...
light that surrounds you...

Ki Im'kha M'kor Hayyim... for with You is the source of Life.
B'Orcka Nireh Or... In Your light we see light...[8]

2. Remember something in your life, something that happened recently, for which you would like to say thanks.
   Breathe in... and breathe out...
   Keep thinking about that special event, remembering how grateful you were.
   Breathe in... and breathe out...
   Add other blessings for which you want to give thanks.
   Breathe in... and breathe out ... (repeat)
   Modim Anachnu Lakh... We give thanks to You (our God)

3. See if you can get your body very still, very quiet.
   Breathe in... and breathe out...
   Listen to the sound of your own breathing. Listen to the quietness inside of you.
   Breathe in... and breathe out...
   Imagine all of Israel listening to the *Shema.*
   Imagine all of Israel as one.
   Breathe in... and breathe out...
   You are listening to what God wants you to do in the world.
   You are feeling at one with God.
   Shema Yisrael Adonai Eloheinu Adonai Ehad... Listen Israel. Adonai is our God; Adonai is One.

[8] A meditation by Joe Rosenstein from *Siddur Eit Ratzon*, p. 9, Shiviti Publications, Highland Park, NJ, 2003. Used with permission.

4. With younger students, you may wish to do a simplified guided meditation. For example:

   Close your eyes and take a slow, deep breath. Breathe in... and breathe out...

   Pretend that you are waking up in the morning in total darkness... Now imagine the sun coming out... You are happy because we count on the sun for light, for warmth, and for growing food... You are very grateful... You want to say a prayer to thank God for the light.

Then you introduce the prayer *Ha-Meir La-Aretz* or introduce a unit on reciting blessings.

Skill Development

One of the most important goals of Jewish education today is the acquisition of basic reading and language skills. There are many other skills students learn along the way, from shaking *lulavim* to learning how to chant Torah and Haftarah. When students are struggling to learn new skills and improve existing ones, they need to practice them effectively and to obtain useful feedback. The strategies that follow represent different ways to develop skills. Some are intense and some are fun.

38. Practice-Rehearsal Pairs

Overview

This is a simple strategy for practicing and rehearsing any skill or procedure with a learning partner. The goal is to ensure that both partners can perform the skill or procedure.

Procedure

1. Select a set of skills or procedures you want students to master. Create pairs. Within each pair, assign two roles: 1) explainer or demonstrator and 2) checker.
2. The explainer or demonstrator explains and/or demonstrates how to perform a specified skill or procedure. The checker verifies that the explanation and/or demonstration is correct, encourages, and provides coaching, if needed.
3. The partners reverse roles. The new explainer/demonstrator is given another skill or procedure to perform.
4. The process continues until all the skills are rehearsed.

Variations

1. Use a multi-step skill or procedure (e.g., putting on *tefillin*) instead of a set of several distinct ones. Have the explainer/demonstrator perform one step and have the partner perform the next step until the sequence of steps is completed.
2. When the pairs have completed their work, arrange a demonstration before the class.

Examples

This technique would work well in practicing:

- Hebrew letters
- any prayer
- the Four Questions
- vocabulary words
- parts in a play
- conjugation of verbs
- Hebrew writing—manuscript or cursive
- trope—Torah or Haftorah
- lists—books of the Bible, days of the week, the Hebrew months, *parshiot*

39. Clothesline

Overview

This activity is useful to teach sequencing. It enables students to actively learn the order of items or events. It also provides a way of testing students, since they demonstrate their knowledge before the class.

Procedure

1. Hand out colorful 11" x 18" sheets of paper. Each sheet has a different item written on it. (All the items, when properly arranged, form a sequence (e.g., the Hebrew months of the year.)
2. Ask two volunteers to hold up a clothesline (8' to 10' feet long).
3. Invite the students with the sheets to come forward and place them on the clothesline (with clothespins) in the correct order.
4. The remaining students in the class are asked to act as coaches, helping those who are having trouble finding the correct places.

Variation

Students are paired and given a list of (or cards with) jumbled items. They are asked to put these items in the correct order.

Examples

1. Students are given a list of prayers (e.g .*Amidah, Barkhu, Aleinu, Mah Tovu, Shema, Kaddish*, and *Adon Olam)*. They are asked to put the prayers in the order in which they appear in the service. (Note that the *Kaddish* can be placed in more than one spot. Creating a challenge can provide an additional learning opportunity.)

2. Students are given the names of biblical characters: Esther, Rebecca, Hulda, Miriam, and Deborah. Then they are asked to put them in the order in which they appear in the Bible.
3. Students are asked to put the names of the Five Books of Moses in order. This can be done in English or Hebrew.
4. Students are given the names of holidays (e.g., Pesach, Hanukkah, Tu B'shvat, Sukkot, and Purim). Their task is to place them in historical order, or in the order in which they appear on the Jewish calendar.
5. Hebrew or English letters can be arranged to form a word, such as *shalom*.
6. Give younger students signs or pictures with what was created on days one to seven. Ask them to place the signs or pictures in the order of the creation story.
7. Students can be asked to place the letters of the Hebrew alphabet in the correct order. (Note that one does not have to do all of the letters at one time. You could do this activity with younger children by using only three to six letters.)

40. Rapid Fire

Overview

This is a lively, fast-moving format that can be used for a variety of purposes, such as testing and role-playing. It features continually rotating pairs. Students get the opportunity to respond to rapidly fired questions or other types of challenges.

Procedure

1. Decide on the purpose for which you would like to use rapid fire. Here are some examples when your goal is skill development:
   - Students can test or drill each other.
   - Students can role-play a situation assigned to them.
   - Students can teach each other.

   You can also use this strategy for other situations. Examples:
   - Students can interview others to obtain their views and opinions.
   - Students can discuss a short text or quotation.
2. Arrange chairs in two facing rows. Have enough chairs for all the students in the class.
3. Separate the chairs into clusters of three to five on each side or row. The arrangement might look like this:

4. Distribute to each x student a card containing a task or assignment to which he or she will instruct the y person opposite him or her to respond. **You should give a different card to each x member of a cluster.**

   For example: If the goal is to review key prayer words in *Adon Olam*, then each x in a cluster receives a different Hebrew word from that prayer to present to each member of the y cluster. Each member of the y cluster must read the Hebrew word correctly and tell its meaning. (The transliteration and translation can be put on the back of each sheet given to each x in a cluster.)

5. Begin the first assignment. After a brief period of time, announce that it is time for all the y's to rotate one chair to the left (or right) within the cluster. Do not rotate the x's. Have the x person "fire" his or her assignment or task to the y person opposite him or her. Continue for as many rounds as there are tasks. This will depend on how many students there are in the room and in each cluster.

Variations

1. Reverse roles so that the x students become the y students.
2. In some situations it may be interesting and appropriate to give the same assignment to each cluster member. In this instance, the y student will be asked to respond to the same instructions for each member of his or her cluster. For example, a student could translate the same word (e.g., *tov*) more than once or could be asked to role-play the same situation a number of times.

Examples

1. Have students test each other (e.g., ask the person opposite you to tell you the meaning of the vocabulary word on his or her flashcard, such as *eparon, near, gir, kisai, shulhan*).
2. Have students question each other (e.g., ask the person opposite him or her "What did Mordecai do in the story of Purim? Ahashverosh? Vashti? Haman? Esther?").
3. Have students interview each other (e.g., ask the opposite person his or her opinion about the importance of keeping kosher, not driving on Shabbat, fasting on Tisha B'Av, avoiding gossiping, not eating *hometz* on Pesah).

4. Have students give each other a character to role-play (e.g., ask the person opposite to portray a person who has just arrived from Eastern Europe at the turn of the century and needs directions to Hester street, followed by buying pickles, applying for a job, getting on a streetcar, complaining to a landlord about the lack of heat).
5. Have students teach each other (e.g., ask the person opposite to teach when to use a *sh'va na* and when to use a *sh'va nah*; when does a *vav* have the sound of the letter v; when does a *vav* have the sound of oh or oo; what letters have a *dagesh*; what letters are "silent"?).

41. Creative Role-Playing

Overview

Role-play is activity that dramatizes events and issues or allows students to practice skills. There are endless ways to do role-playing to fit virtually any classroom situation. Here are some creative options.

Procedure

1. Begin by having students coach you in a role-play. It reduces the threat of role-playing by placing the teacher in the lead role and involving the class in providing the responses and setting the scenario's direction. Create a role-play, such as Esther pleading to save the Jews. Inform the class that you will play the leading role in the role-play. The students' job is to help you deal with the situation. Obtain a student volunteer to role-play the other person in the situation (e.g., King Ahashveirosh). Give that student an opening script to read to help him or her get into the role. Start the role-play but stop frequently and ask the class to give you feedback and direction as the scenario progresses. Don't hesitate to ask students to provide specific lines for you to utilize. For example, at a specific point say, "What should I say next?" Listen to suggestions from the audience and try one of them. Continue the role-play so that students increasingly coach you on how to handle the situation.
2. Make role-playing safe by doing it in pairs. Pair students and give them a role-playing scenario to act out together without public scrutiny. Arrange enough private space so that student pairs can role-play simultaneously. There is no guarantee that every pair will take the assignment seriously, but more will than will not, especially if they may be asked to perform later on in front of the class. After simultaneous role-playing you can invite students to

perform in front of the entire class, now that they have had time to practice. At this time you can act as a skill coach, giving pointers and demonstrating new behaviors.

3. Use scripts. If you want a way to show students effective skills and yet make them feel safe, give them scripts to read that contain successful ways to handle situations. At first they can simply read the scripts, with different students playing different characters. (You can also have students read scripts in pairs.) As the students learn effective approaches, challenge them to put the scripts away and try the situation without them. Or you can invite students to write their own scripts.

4. Introduce whole-class role-playing by rotating parts. Once students are on stage before their peers, the pressure builds. A way to ease students into this format is to rotate the actors rapidly. For example, assume that you have a student who is asked to stand up to peer pressure. You might obtain one or two volunteers to portray the pressuring peers. They can remain in this role throughout the role-play. The person under pressure can be given one shot at responding, and then another student can take over for him or her. You can involve several students in this role-play, none of whom has to be on stage very long.

Now that students have rehearsed in their minds how they would act in a specific situation, invite them to plan how they might actually act on their thoughts.

Variation

Younger students can role-play characters by pantomiming as you narrate. Or have them tell their own version of a story (e.g., Purim *Megillah*) on a tape recorder that will play as puppets they create do the acting.

Examples

Below are several scenes that your students can role-play.

1. You are Abraham. The student is Eliezer. (You are asking him to find a wife for Isaac.)

2. You are Moses. The student is a taskmaster. (You see him oppressing a slave.)

3. You are Devorah. The student is Barak. (You are requesting that he lead the battle.)
4. You are God. The student is Cain. (You are inquiring about his brother, Abel.)
5. You are Mordecai. The student is Esther. (You are persuading her to save her people.)
6. You are a person asked by a Christian, "What do you think of Jesus Christ?" Your student is the Christian posing the question.
7. You are Joseph. One student portrays a baker and the second a butler. You are asked to interpret their dreams.
8. You are Judah Maccabee. Two students portray Jews of the period. (You are trying to persuade them to fight against the soldiers of Antiochus.)
9. You are H̲annah. The student is Eli. (You are explaining your behavior to him.)
10. You are Moses. The student is Pharaoh. (You want Pharaoh to let the Israelites leave Egypt.)
11. You are God. The student is Abraham. You are telling Abraham to leave his home for an unknown place.
12. You are a student in a class. A child has just moved o the community. You are welcoming him or her to the class (*hakhnasat orh̲im*).

42. Silent Demonstration

Overview

This is a strategy to use when you are teaching any kind of step-by-step procedure. By demonstrating a procedure as silently as possible, you encourage students to be mentally alert.

Procedure

1. Decide on a multi-step procedure you want students to learn (e.g., rolling a Torah scroll).
2. Ask the students to watch you perform the entire procedure. Just do it, with little or no explanation or commentary about what and why you are doing what you do. Give them a visual glimpse of the big picture or the entire job. Do not expect retention. At this point you are merely establishing readiness for learning.
3. Form pairs. Demonstrate the first part of the procedure, again with little or no explanation or commentary. **Ask pairs to discuss with each other what they observed you doing.** (Telling them what you are doing will lessen the mental alertness of students.) Obtain a volunteer to explain what you did. If the students have difficulty, demonstrate again. Acknowledge correct observations.
4. Have the pairs practice with each other the first part of the procedure. When it is mastered, proceed with a silent demonstration of the next parts of the procedure, followed by paired practice.

5. End by challenging students to do the entire procedure without any help.

Variations

1. If possible, give students an opening task to attempt the procedure before any demonstration. Encourage guesses and a freedom to make mistakes. By doing this, you will immediately get students mentally involved. Then have them watch you demonstrate.
2. If some students master the procedure sooner than others, recruit them as silent demonstrators.

Examples

Below are a variety of procedures you can teach using this method.

1. Putting on *tefillin*
2. Lighting candles on a *menorah*
3. Braiding *hallah* dough
4. Bowing during *Aleinu*
5. Writing cursive Hebrew letters
6. Wearing a *tallit*
7. Shaking a *lulav*
8. Finding the *shoresh* in a Hebrew word

43. Active Hebrew Reading Practice

Overview

The criteria for successful fluent reading activity are maximum drill, efficient use of time, and the participation of every child. Learning activities should increase skill but never embarrass students. What follows are a series of active learning strategies that accomplish this.

Procedure

1. Make sure lines are numbered on the page from which your students are reading. If yours are not numbered, have students do this before each lesson. It will help them to quickly find certain words on the page, giving them more reading practice.
2. Make sure **you** say each word (correctly) to introduce it. Otherwise a student's mistake may stick in other students' minds.
3. Decide in advance how to deal with students' mistakes. Simple mistakes, such as one incorrect vowel or consonant, can be corrected on the spot. However, if a student is stammering over a letter or word or makes several errors, it may be better to say *shalom* or allow the student to pass. This will be a signal to move on to another reader without a big fuss and also to let the student know you will return to him or her (perhaps in small-group or seat-work time) to assist him/her. If several students have made similar mistakes, this is a signal to you to review, as well as to make remediation sheets for those having problems.
4. Explain to students why drills and practice are so important. Let them know that if they work at this with you, they will be pleased

that they've accomplished something. Let them know that you will try to make the drills as interesting as possible and that you'll use various techniques to do this. Tell them that you will also be adding games and activities to enliven the class. (Keep your promise!)

5. If you are practicing reading prayers, use a text or a sheet that you have duplicated. Save the prayer books for a real prayer service or the recitation of blessings for appropriate occasions.
6. The group will always read better than its individual members. The group moves individuals along. That's okay (that's what happens at synagogue!), but that means that you need to have both group and individual recitation.

Examples

1. Learning new or difficult words:
   - Get students involved by having them look over lines and select words they think are troubling or of which they are not sure. (You can ask them to choose words that they think others would find difficult.) These words can be boxed. Students then raise their hands to indicate a difficult word, identifying by line and word (e.g., "line four, word three"). You ask the rest of the students to find that word and put a finger below it. Next you say the word slowly and clearly and have the class repeat the word.
   - Designate a difficult word in advance and have students mark it. You read the word, then a student is asked to read that word and the one after it. A second student reads the word and the two words after it, and so on, up to five words. This enables the class to hear the new or difficult word at least six times.
   - To practice difficult words, use the gamelike technique of guessing a word (e.g., "I'm thinking of a word on line ________"). Another variation is for you to read the word before or after and have the students find the correct word.
   - A fun way for younger students to practice difficult words is for you to whisper them and have the students read your lips. Then have the students locate them on designated lines (e.g., "Can you locate [the word just whispered] on line five?").
2. Reinforcing phonic recognition—reading by syllables

- Sound out the syllables of a word. For example, the first syllable would be *e*, the second would be *pa*, and the third would be *ron*. Then the class reads the whole word together: *eparon*.
- Accumulate sound elements. For example, the first student says *e*, the second says *epa*, and the third says *eparon*. Have the class repeat the word.
- You say the first sound and the students read the whole word. For example, you say *ba* and they read (in unison) *baruch*.
- To teach them to follow along with their eyes, play "Catch Me." This gamelike activity requires you to read syllables or words slowly and clearly (for younger students, you can read just letters). Students follow along, pointing to each word or syllable. Occasionally you can make a mistake on purpose. The students will then call out *lo!* and read the correct version.
- For extra credit or homework, give students English words written in Hebrew. These can be words they would enjoy decoding (e.g., favorite teams, songs, foods). Challenge your better students to make up these sheets for the class. Just make sure you check them carefully before they are distributed or sent home.

3. Strengthening whole-word identification—rhythm reading
   - You read the first word and the class (in unison) reads the next, and so on.
   - The students read the first word and you read the next.
   - Read around the room (without calling names). The first student reads one word, the second reads two words, the third reads three words, and so on.
   - Call students to read by subgroups. For example, "All those with blue on today, read line one. All those wearing sneakers, read line six." Note: avoid calling girls or boys to read a line. This only promotes separation and competition between the sexes. Try to make categories fun, such as "those who love pizza, those who play video games," etc.
4. Developing fluent reading
   - Duplicate the prayer your class is studying and add commas or periods in the appropriate places. (Eliminate this step if your text has these.) Have each student read until he or she reaches a comma or period.

- Have students work in pairs, coaching each other (helping, correcting, and encouraging as needed). Circulate to make sure mistakes are not ignored.

5. Improving accurate and fluent reading
   - Use choral reading as a technique. Have three students at a time be leaders and the rest of the class be the chorus. Each leader is given one line to read (with some time to practice and be checked by you). The student then reads the line, and the chorus echoes it. When all three leaders have had a turn they join the chorus, and three new leaders are selected, A variation is to have all three read the lines together, and the class echoes.
   - Students work in pairs using a tape or CD (that you, the cantor, or a parent volunteer has made) to check if they are reading/singing correctly.
   - To improve speed, have students set their own goals (giving them some ownership in the learning process). These goals can change as students become more proficient. Have a class celebration when all students have achieved their goals. (Their goals should be private and not posted.) You will need a stopwatch for this activity.

6. Games for reviewing
   - Put review words on the board and number them. Toss a Koosh ball (or larger ball for younger students) to a student and call out a number. If the student catches the ball, he or she reads the word and tosses the ball to another student, calling out a different number.
   - Write numbers on each section of an egg carton. Have students toss a penny or button into the egg carton. Have them read the word that's on the board with that number.
   - Make a Bingo card for each student. You will need twenty-four squares plus one free space. Have children write a different word or letter in each space, using pre-selected words. Call out the letters or words from a corresponding pile of cards. Use pennies or buttons for makers. The first student to fill his or her card wins.
   - Before class, place flash cards or signs with review words at various spots in the room (e.g., the walls, door, window, floor,

even the ceiling). Or let the student who arrives first help you do this. Dim the lights and take out a bright flashlight. Shine the flashlight on a word that you've placed in the room. Call on a student to read the word. If he or she is correct, that student can take the flashlight, shine it on the next word, and call on the next student to read. Continue until every child has had a chance to read and shine the flashlight.[9]

[9]A technique taught by Susan Weiner Reiman.

Computer-Mediated Learning[10]

With the advent of computers as basic educational tools, a whole new world has opened in Jewish education. Students can learn Hebrew skills at their own pace and with a choice of learning aids by working with a multimedia tutorial program. A group of students can take virtual Jewish field trips utilizing a wide variety of online resources, including maps, photos, interactive activities, and video clips. Students can collaborate with other students throughout the world as they email one another, and a class can display its accomplishments on its own website.

The teacher who does not use the internet or ignores its power is out of touch with his/her students' lives. These days children use computers from the time they are about three years old, and they never stop.

[10] All the internet sources for this section were provided by Nancy Messinger, Director of Educational Resources, Auerbach CAJE, Philadelphia. Nancy also provided valuable ideas for this section.

44 • Virtual Field Trips

Overview

One of the joys of the web is that it can take students to many places via virtual field trips. There are Jewish virtual field trips you can have your students experience that will provide them with exciting visual and textual information that would not be attainable otherwise.

Procedure

1. You may choose to start off by taking an online course and learning how to plan a virtual field trip. Go to *www.jecc.org/edres/medtech/vft/home.htm*.
2. Find a website that provides a virtual field trip of interest to your students (see examples below for suggestions). Examine the website yourself to identify what it contains. Some may merely have photos. Others may have textual information and discussion questions or learning activities. Best of all are sites that allow your students to interact directly with the site.
3. If you want some of these elements (e.g., text information, learning activities, etc.), and they are lacking, provide them directly to your students. For example, you may be able to find information in *The Jewish Encyclopedia*.
4. Decide among these options:
   - Have students independently take a virtual field trip of their choice and ask them to share with classmates their experiences and discoveries.

- Place students in small groups (two to four students) and ask them to collaborate on a group report to be shared with the class.
- Find a way for every student to share one virtual field trip (if sufficient computer resources are available in your school or students use their home computers) and then debrief the experience as a class.

Variation

Do not stop with taking students on field trips in the classroom or assigning students to view field trips as part of an individual or group assignment. Students can create their own virtual field trips of local historical sites or even of their school. Once they see a few field-trip sites, they will understand how to design their own sites. With a digital camera and a bit of practice, students can create excellent projects.

Examples

1. Students can go through the Anne Frank House in Holland at http://www.annefrank.nl/eng/afn/afn.html.
2. Have your students take the Jerusalem Temple tunnel tour at www.aish.com/seminars/tunnel/tour. They can see the *Kotel* at any time of day at www.kotelcam.org and even send a prayer to be placed in the wall.
3. Several Jewish museums present selected collections on the web as well. Tour the Museum of American Jewish History's postcard exhibit at www.nmajh.org/exhibitions/postcards/cards/index.htm and the United States Holocaust Memorial Museum's online exhibitions at www.ushmm.org.
4. A tour of Jerusalem is available at www.md.huje.ad.il/vit.

45. Jewish WebQuests

Overview

A WebQuest is a focused internet project. It helps students to become creative researchers rather than simply surfing from one site to another. Students are given a task in which some or all of the information used by them is drawn from the web. WebQuests are designed to use students' time well, focusing on using information rather than on looking for it, and to support analysis, synthesis, and evaluation. Answers or solutions are not predefined and therefore must be discovered or created by students.

Procedure

1. Begin by going to a list of Jewish WebQuests at www.jecc.org. You can also search for sample secular WebQuests to give you ideas and, occasionally, one you might find appropriate for your students. Go to webquest.sdsu.edu/webquest.html or www.schooldiscovery.com/schrockguide/webquest/webquest.html.
2. You can also create your own. Make note of what you like about existing WebQuests and incorporate those ideas. According to Bernie Dodge, the originator of the WebQuest concept, there are six parts to an effective WebQuest:
   - *Introduction*: orients students and captures their interest
   - *Task*: the end product expected of students
   - *Process*: the strategies students should use to complete the task
   - *Resources*: the websites students will use to complete the task
   - *Evaluation*: how the results of the activity will be measured

- *Conclusion*: a summary of the activity and encouragement to reflect on its process and results

Some examples of webquest tasks include:

- solving mysteries
- creating an oral (with media) presentation
- responding to a case problem
- developing a mission statement
- constructing something
- conducting an experiment

Examples

An excellent WebQuest on Anne Frank can be found at

- http://www.plain.k.12.in.is/hschool/webq/webq11/afrank.htm.
- A WebQuest on *The Prince of Egypt* is available at www.acaje.org/educational/Resources/WebquestPoE.shtml.
- Torah Tots (www.torahtots.com) has printable coloring and puzzle pages about prayer and Torah and detailed, fun Torah synopses for younger children.

46. Email Pen Pals

Overview

Students can share and compare their experiences and learning with other students anywhere in the world. Email pen pals can be entire classes or individual students.

Procedure

1. Begin by becoming an email pal with another teacher before involving your students. Suggest what you might have your students write to each other about. Options include:
   - personal information and biographies
   - information about the school or synagogue
   - sharing about learning activities in the respective schools
   - exchanges about Jewish family practices (e.g., upcoming holidays)
   - interviewing each other
   - ideas for joint projects, such as developing a survey and comparing results
2. Once you work out a mutual plan, do a pilot run. (You and your pen pal should select an assignment that is simple before trying anything complicated.)
3. Run the pilot. If students are using their home computers, check that all of them had a smooth experience.
4. When e-palling with Israel, take note of issues such as language level, age, and religious orientation.

Examples

1. To find out how students can do projects with other students in their classes as well as with students in other schools, other cities, and other countries, see Global Schoolhouse E-pals at www.globalschoolhouse.org.
2. The Joint Authority for Jewish Zionist Education has a pen pal program entitled "Building a Jewish World" at http://www.jewish-world.org.il.
3. The Ghetto Fighters House in Israel's class-to-class book reading and review email project called International Book Sharing Project can be found at www.gfh.org.il.

47. Class Websites

Overview

Your class can create its own website. The pride of displaying the creative writings of students, their artwork, or any other visual outcome of their classroom learning is something that can motivate students to want to learn more and achieve results.

Procedure

1. The easiest way to get going is to create a specific class area on an existing website, such as a synagogue website. To insure security, be sure to password-protect the area and have students use pen names.

2. Teachers and their students can:
   - post class newsletters, students' PowerPoint projects, and class assignments.
   - scan completed student artwork and written work onto a special class section on the website.
   - post links that will help the students with their studies, such as fun Hebrew sites.
   - develop a pen pal area with a class from Israel (exchange photos and work on joint projects).
   - create web assignments for which students can post their answers.
   - highlight class *tikkun olam* projects on the site and include links so relatives can make donations in their honor online.
3. If your school has a computer lab, allow students to work on their own independent website in class.

4. Encourage parents (and grandparents) to access the website to see their children's work.

Examples

1. Organize the website around the Jewish calendar. As each holiday approaches, change the content under categories such as:
   - historical background
   - observance and celebrations
   - contemporary lessons
   - recipes
   - objects and symbols
2. Organize the website around a theme. Change the theme during the year. Themes may include:
   - *tikkun olam*
   - *tzedakah*
   - *tefillah*
   - *kashrut*
   - Shabbat

SECTION 4 How to Make Learning Unforgettable

Some teachers teach until the final moments of a school term, semester, or course of study. They think that at the last minute they can cram in more information and cover topics and material that are still on their agendas. The value of covering any subject is suspect. To cover means to hide, to disguise, and, in some cases, to scatter about. The urge to teach until the end often leads to hiding, disguising, and scattering about. When learning is active, there is an opportunity to understand. When time is taken to consolidate what has been learned, there is an opportunity to retain.

Think for a moment what happens when you work hard at a computer, retrieving information, solving problems, and composing thoughts... but you fail to save the work you've done. Yep, it's all gone. Learning can fall victim to that dreaded event as well, if students are not given the chance to save what they have learned.

Besides saving what has been learned, it's important to savor it. Like any experience, learning is savored when there is a chance to reflect on it and give it some emotional closure. Just as we have spoken of the "appetizer" and entree" portions of active learning, we now can consider the "desert."

There are many positive actions you can take to bring your class to a meaningful and perhaps even unforgettable close. In this section we will consider them in three categories.

Reviewing Strategies

This part deals with ways to help students recall what they have learned and test their current knowledge and ability. You will find reviewing strategies that engage students and help them save the learning they have acquired.

Self-Assessment

This part deals with ways to help students assess what they know now, what they can do now, and what attitudes they hold now. You will find assessment strategies that help students evaluate their progress.

Shalom, L'hitraot

This part deals with ways to help students reminisce about their experiences together and express appreciation. You will find strategies that help to bring closure to the class and enable students to say goodbye.

Reviewing Strategies

One of the surest ways to make learning stick is to include time for reviewing what's been learned. In fact, material that's been reviewed by students is five times more likely to be retained than material that has not. That's because reviewing allows students to reconsider the information and find ways to store it in their brains. What follows is an array of strategies to promote review. In addition to being active, they all make reviewing fun.

48. Index Card Match

Overview

This is an active, fun way to review class material. It allows students to pair up and quiz their classmates.

Procedure

1. Write down on separate index cards questions about anything taught in the class. Create enough question cards to equal half the number of students. (Other options are cards containing words and their definitions or any other pairing in which two cards need to be matched.)
2. On separate cards, write answers to each of these questions.
3. Mix the two sets of cards and shuffle them several times so that they are well mixed.
4. Give one card to each student. Explain that this is a matching exercise. Some students have review questions, and others have the answers.
5. Have students find matching cards. When a match is formed, ask the matching students to find seats together. (Tell them not to reveal to other students what is on their cards.)
6. When all the matching pairs have been seated, have each pair quiz the rest of the class by reading aloud their question and challenging classmates to tell them the answer.

Variations

1. Develop cards containing a sentence with a missing word to be matched to cards containing the missing word. For example, "Elijah the ______ visits Jewish homes at the Passover seder" (Prophet).
2. Instead of using index cards, tear sheets of pape, so that each is different. Put the review question on one half of the paper and the answer on the other half. Students will know immediately if theirs is a match because the two half-sheets will fit together like an *afikomen*.

Examples

Here are a variety of situations in which cards can be matched:

- key Hebrew words and translations
- beginnings and endings of prayers
- holidays and appropriate blessings
- foods and appropriate blessings
- names of prayers and themes of prayers (e.g., *V'ahavta* and love, *ha-Meir la-Aretz* and light)
- for younger students, pictures of Jewish symbols and their corresponding holidays
- block printing of letters or words and the same words in cursive writing
- names of holidays and the Hebrew months in which the holidays occur
- names of biblical characters and their attributes (e.g., Rebecca and *kindness to people and animals*, Abraham and *hospitality*, Moses and *leadership*, Esther and *courage)*
- for younger students, biblical characters and their associated holidays
- articles from the headlines matched with cards (or pictures) of how we can be God's partner in such situations[11]

[11]Suggested by Rabbi Richie Fagan.

49. Crossword Puzzle

Overview

Designing a review test as a crossword puzzle invites immediate engagement and participation. A crossword puzzle can be completed individually or in teams.

Procedure

1. The first step is to brainstorm several key terms or names related to the course of study you have completed.
2. Construct a simple crossword puzzle including as many of these items as you can. Darken spaces you do not need. (Note: If it is too difficult to create a crossword puzzle with these items, include fun items unrelated to the class as fillers.)
3. Create clues for your crossword items. Use any of the following kinds:
   - a short definition ("adorning a ritual object to make it more beautiful": *hiddur mitzvah)*
   - a category in which the item fits ("*Baruch Sh'amar*": prayer)
   - an example ("honoring your parents is an example of this: *mitzvah)*
   - an opposite ("the opposite of *or*": *choshech)*
4. Distribute the puzzle to students, either individually or in teams.
5. Set a time limit. Award a prize to the individual or team that has the most correct items.

Variations

1. Have the entire group work cooperatively to complete the crossword puzzle.
2. Simplify the puzzle by deciding on one word that has been key to the entire lesson. Write it in horizontal crossword squares. Use words that summarize other points in the lesson and fit them vertically into the key word.

Example

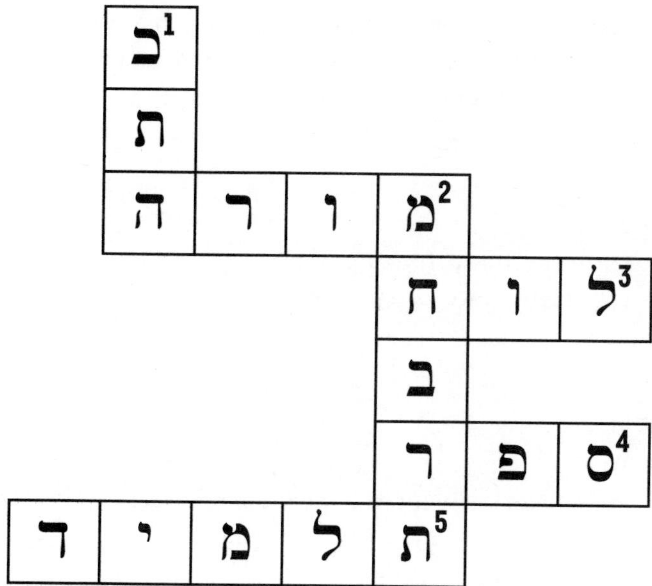

Down
1. class
2. notebook

Across
2. teacher
3. chalkboard
4. book
5. students

50. Jewpardy

Overview

This strategy is designed like the popular TV game show Jeopardy. The answers are given, and the challenge is to come up with the correct question. The format can easily be used as a review of course material.

Procedure

1. Create three to four categories of review questions. Use any of the following generic categories:
   - Concepts or ideas
   - Facts
   - Skills
   - Names

   Or create categories by topic. For example, a class on Hebrew might involve topics such as Months, Numbers, and Colors.
2. Develop at least three answers (and their corresponding questions) per category. For example, the answer "This color joins *kohol* on the flag of the State of Israel" can be matched to the question "What is *lavan*?" You don't need to have the same number of questions/answers in each category. However, you should develop questions and answers of increasing difficulty.
3. Make a Jeopardy game board on a large piece of paper. Announce the categories and the point values for each category. Below is a sample game board.

Months	Colors	Numbers
10 points	10 points	10 points
20 points	20 points	20 points
30 points	30 points	30 points

4. Form teams of three to six students and provide a responder card for each team. If possible, create groups with a range of skill or knowledge levels.
5. Ask teams to choose a team captain and team scorekeeper.
   - **Team captains** represent the team. They are the only ones who can hold up the responder card and give an answer. **Team captains must confer with the team before giving an answer.**
   - **Scorekeepers** are responsible for adding and subtracting points for their team.

   Note: As the game moderator, you are responsible for keeping track of which questions have been asked. As each question is used, cross it off the game board. Put a check mark next to any questions students had difficulty answering. You can come back to these questions when the game is over.
6. Review the following rules of the game:
   - The team captain who holds up the responder card first gets the opportunity to answer.
   - All answers must be given in the form of a question.
   - If the correct response is given, the point value for that category is awarded. If the response is incorrect, the point value is deducted from the team's score, and the other teams have an opportunity to answer.
   - The team that gives the last correct response controls the board.

Variations

1. Instead of using team captains, have each member of the team take a turn playing Jewpardy. He or she can or cannot consult with team members before answering.
2. Have students create Jewpardy questions.

Instead of the first one who holds up a card responding, simply rotate from one group to the next. This is a better way to play the game when you have one or two students who can always respond first.

Examples

1. "What is *haroset?*" is the question for "Something chopped on a seder plate."
2. "Who is Korakh?" is the question for "The man who led a rebellion against Moses."
3. "Who is Aaron?" is the question for "He built the golden calf."
4. "What is 'Thou shall not bear false witness'?" is the question for "This is the ninth of the Ten Commandments."
5. "What is the Talmud?" is the question for "A vast collection of commentaries on the Mishnah."
6. "What are apples and honey?" is the question for "This is a sweet treat on Rosh ha-Shanah."
7. "What is the dove?" is the question for "This animal, when it did not return, told Noah that there was dry land."
8. "Who is David Ben Gurion?" is the question for "He was the first Prime Minister of Israel."
9. "What is an orange?" is the question for "This fruit is a new item on the seder plate."
10. "What is the ark?" is the question for "This is where animals came two by two."

Self-Assessment

The end of a term, semester, or course of study is a time for reflection. What have I learned? What do I now believe? What are my skills? What do I need to improve? Allowing time for self-assessment gives students the opportunity to examine what the class has meant or done for them. The strategies that follow are structured ways to promote this kind of self-assessment. They also provide meaningful closure to the class experience.

51. Rate Yourself

Overview

Allowing time for self-assessment gives students the opportunity to examine what the course or unit has meant to them. The suggestions that follow are structured ways of promoting this type of self-assessment.

Procedure

1. Prepare a survey in which students rate themselves on items that reflect the learning they have acquired. You can ask them to evaluate such things as:
   - the skills they have mastered (e.g., how well they can read the Hebrew alphabet).
   - the information they've acquired (e.g., how informed they are about the founding of the State of Israel).
   - The concepts, topics, or ideas they have understood (e.g., how well they understand the concept of *kibbud av v'aim* [honoring parents] or *hachnasat orchcim* [welcoming guests]).
   - New or expanded areas of interest (e.g., how interested they are in learning more about different denominations in Judaism).
2. Make the survey user-friendly by using simple devices such as:
   - Checklist (e.g., Check the skill areas below in which you have improved: *trope* for High Holidays, *nusach* for Shabbat, reading Hebrew)
   - Rating scale (e.g., Rate your understanding of how Judaism differs from Christianity: poor, fair, good, excellent)
   - Sentence completion (e.g., One topic from our class that I still I think about a lot is ___________)

- Short answer (e.g., What's the topic we studied this year about which you've increased your knowledge the most?)

3. Invite students to assess how they have changed. For example, ask such questions as:
   - How has studying *Torah* benefited you?
   - Rate your ability to *daven musaf*:
     - ☐ excellent
     - ☐ good
     - ☐ fair
     - ☐ poor
4. It's important that students are honest with themselves. They will be if you make the survey something they complete only for themselves. At the same time, consider having students share those responses they want to reveal with a partner or in a small group of students.

Example

Here is an assessment designed for fifth graders.

1. I read Hebrew well.

1	2	3
strongly disagree	not sure	strongly agree

2. I understand what the prayer means. (check each item)

   ______*Shema*

   ______*Kedusha*

   ______*Aleinu*

   ______*Ashrei*

3. My ability to write Hebrew letters is ____________________.
4. Which holidays do you know the most about?

   Which holidays do you know the least about?

52. • Gallery of Learning

Overview

This activity is a way to assess and celebrate what students have learned over a course of study.

Procedure

1. Divide students into groups of two to four members.
2. Ask each subgroup to discuss what they are taking away from the class. This may include any of the following:
   - new knowledge (e.g., prophets of ancient Israel)
   - new skills (e.g., Hebrew reading)
   - improvement (e.g., in Torah *trope*)
   - new or renewed interest (e.g., in learning to speak Hebrew)
   - confidence (e.g., in *davening* skills)
3. Then ask them to list these learnings on large sheets of paper. Request that they title the list "What We Are Taking Away".
4. Paper the walls with these lists.
5. Ask students to walk by each list. Request that each person place a check next to learnings on lists other than his or her own that he or she is taking away as well.
6. Survey the results, noting the most popular learnings. Also mention some that are unusual and unexpected.

Variations

1. If the size of the class warrants, ask each student to make his or her own list.

2. Instead of listing learnings, ask students to list "keepers." Keepers are ideas or suggestions given in the class that students think are worth keeping or retaining for future application (e.g., the best way to practice *trope*).

Examples

1. The following list is the result of completing the study of the Book of Genesis:

   What We Are Taking Away

   - Giving the firstborn honor and power automatically is not a good idea.
   - You can look at the stories again and again and learn different things.
   - Many characters repeat the same mistakes.
   - The women of Genesis are just as important as the men.

2. The following list is the result of learning the Shabbat morning service:

   What We Are Taking Away

   - It isn't just a bunch of prayers that have no theme.
   - It has a dramatic buildup.
   - It's a good combination of private prayer, communal singing, and congregation-wide *davening*.
   - Some of the prayers fit the modern world really well, and some don't.

53. Learning Fair

Overview

This activity enables the class to demonstrate what they have learned in a celebratory way.

Procedure

1. Upon completion of a unit of study, ask the class to brainstorm ways to demonstrate what they have learned.
2. The class decides which activities to include and who will be responsible for presenting each one. Presentations can include music and art. How many are assigned to each subgroup depends on the size of the class.
3. The class must decide whom to invite (e.g., parents, a younger class) and when to hold the event. (This must be worked out with the school principal or administrator.) Invitations are sent.
4. Each subgroup prepares its presentation for the fair with feedback from the other subgroups.
5. Learning is reinforced as the students review by demonstrating or teaching others.

Variation

The teacher selects the activities. The students are assigned a task or select one from a hat.

Examples

1. Students teach a selection of *Mishna* or *Pirke Avot* to parents.
2. Each subgroup teaches a part of the seder to a younger class.

3. An Israel fair might include activities such as:
    - an area in the social hall that has representations of cities in Israel (with a prepared information guide).
    - a presentation of Israeli singing and/or dancing.
    - a "café" serving Israeli food (e.g., falafel) that the students have learned to make.
    - tables set up to teach about a few charities in Israel that resonated with the students.
    - a large map of Israel that students created to indicate key places.
    - a "museum" of "artifacts that students made with clay.
    - a *shouk* with proceeds going to *tzedakah* in Israel.
    - a *kotel* where guests can insert prayers (these can be written in advance by the students).
    - a "yeshiva" where students teach a short text (e.g., from the week's Torah portion).

54. Assessment Collage

Overview

This exercise uses the activity of making a picture collage to enable students to assess themselves in a creative way.

Procedure

1. Gather several Jewish magazines (especially ones geared to their age group). Have scissors, marking pens, and glue (or tape) available for students.
2. Ask students to create a collage that represents what they have learned.
3. Make the following suggestions:
   - Cut out words from the magazines that describe your current views, skills, or knowledge.
   - Paste in visual images that graphically describe your knowledge or accomplishments.
   - Use marking pens to title the collage and to add your own words or images.
4. Create a gallery of the assessment collages. Invite students to tour the results and comment on the collages displayed.

Variation

If the class is large, have them do this activity in small groups. Then have each small group share their collage with the other groups.

Examples

A collage could include pictures of:

1. Holiday celebrations
2. Ritual objects (such as a *mezzuzah*)
3. Life-cycle events
4. Hebrew letters
5. Historical figures
6. People doing *tzedakah*
7. People doing *g'milut hassadim* (acts of loving kindness)

Shalom, L'hitraot

We hope your students have developed feelings of closeness toward their classmates. This is especially likely if the students have taken part in active learning activities. They need to say goodbye to one another and express final sentiments. The strategies that follow are some good ones.

55. Goodbye Scrabble

Overview

This is a technique that enables students at the end of a class to celebrate together what they have experienced. This is achieved by creating a giant Scrabble board.

Procedure

1. Create a large display of the title of the course or subject matter. Merge the words in the title if there are more than one. For example, "Jewish History" becomes jewishhistory.
2. Give students marking pens. Explain, if necessary, how words can be created in Scrabble fashion using the displayed title as a model. Review that words can be created:
   - horizontally or vertically
   - beginning with, ending with, and incorporating any available letters.

   Remind students, however, that two words cannot merge with each other—there must be a space between them. Permit proper names as words.
3. Set a time limit and invite students to create as many words as they can that are associated with the subject matter or the learning experiences that have taken place.
4. Suggest that they divide the labor so that some students are recording while others are searching for new words.
5. Call time and have the students count the words and applaud the visual record of their experience with one another!

Variations

1. If the group size is unwieldy for this activity, divide the class into subgroups that each create a Scrabble board. Display the results and tally the **total** number of words produced by the entire class.
2. Simplify the activity by writing the course title or subject matter vertically and asking students to write (horizontally) a verb, adjective, or noun that they associate with the title and that begins with each letter or incorporates the letter.

Examples:

1. Here is a scrabble solution for the word PASSOVER:

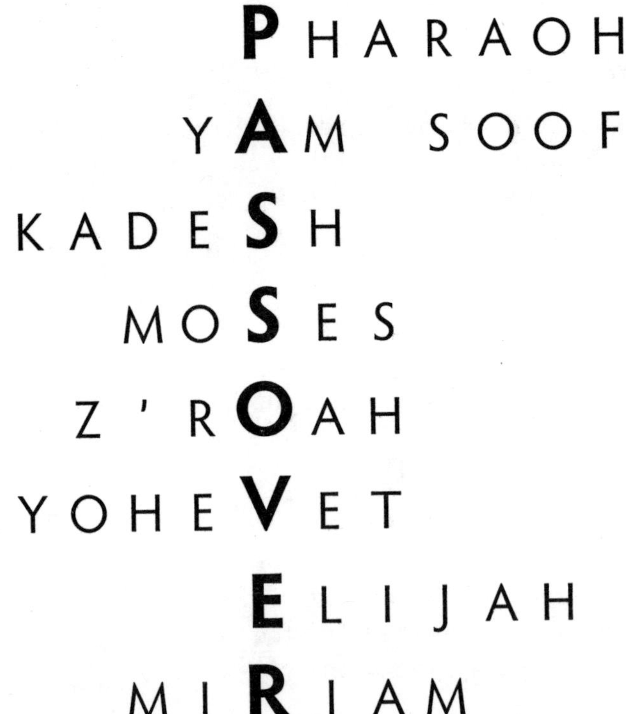

2. Here is a scrabble solution for the word *SHABBAT*:

S HALOM
H APPY
A LL TOGETHER
B EST FOOD
B IMAH
A T REST
T ORAH

56. Connections

Overview

This is an activity that symbolically draws a class to a close. It is especially appropriate when students have formed close connections with one another.

Procedure

1. Use a skein of yard to literally and symbolically connect students.
2. Ask everyone to stand and form a circle. Start the process by stating briefly what you have experienced as a result of teaching the class.
3. Holding on the end of the yarn, toss the skein to a student on the other side of the circle. Ask that person to state briefly what he or she has experienced as a result of participating in the class. Than ask that person to hold on to the yarn and toss the skein to another student.
4. Have each student take a turn at receiving the skein, sharing reflections, and tossing the yarn on, continuing to hold on to his or her piece. The resulting visual is a web of yarn connecting every member of the group.
5. Complete the activity by stating that the class began as a collection of individuals willing to connect and learn from one another.
6. Cut the yarn with scissors so that each person, though departing as an individual, takes a piece of the other students with them. Thank students for their interest, ideas, time, and effort.

Variations

1. Ask each student to express appreciation to the person who tossed him or her the yarn.
2. Instead of using yarn, toss a ball or a similar object. As each person receives the ball, he or she can express final sentiments.

Examples

Comments from students who participated in a bar/bat mitzvah class might include:

- I'm glad I got to know people in the class.
- I thank everyone who came to my bar mitzvah ceremony.
- I had fun in this class.
- I really learned to work hard.
- I want to thank everyone who helped me practice my Haftorah.
- I liked the *tzedakah* projects we did together.
- You helped me be less nervous about getting up on the *bimah*.
- You all have been a great group!

57. • Class Photo

Overview

This is an activity that acknowledges the contributions of every student while celebrating the whole class.

Procedure

1. Assemble students for a class photograph. It's best to create at least three rows—one sitting on the floor, one sitting in chairs, and one standing behind the chairs. As you are about to take their picture, express your own final sentiments. Stress how much active learning depends on the support and involvement of students. Thank students for playing a large part in the success of the class.
2. Then invite one student at a time to leave the group and become the photographer. (Optional: have each participant merely come up and view what a final picture of the class would look like.)
3. If the class is not too large, ask each student to share his or her final thoughts with the group. Ask the group to applaud the student for his/her contributions to the group.
4. Email the photo to each of your students.

Variations

1. Use the photography session as an opportunity to review some of the highlights of the class.
2. Instead of a public disclosure of sentiments, ask students to write final thoughts on sheets of paper taped to the walls.

Example

About the Authors

Dr. Shoshana Silberman (shoshana_silberman@comcast.net) is a consultant at the Auerbach Central Agency for Jewish Education in Philadelphia. She has been a Jewish educator for over forty years as teacher, principal, consultant, and workshop leader.

Shoshana is the author of

The Family Haggadah (Karben, 1987)

The Whole Megillah (Almost!) (Karben, 1990)

Tiku Shofar: A Mahzor for Children and Their Parents (United Synagogue, 1993)

Siddur Shema Yisrael:, A Siddur for Sabbath and Festivals and Sourcebook for Students and Families (United Synagogue, 1996)

The Family Haggadah II (Karben, 1997)

Jewish Rhymes for Family Times (United Synagogue, 2005)

The Jewish World Family Haggadah (ibooks, 2006)

Dr. Mel Silberman (mel1038@comcast.net) is Professor Emeritus of Psychological Studies in Education at Temple University, where he won the Great Teacher Award. He has an international reputation in the field of active learning.

Mel is the author of

The Experience of Schooling (Holt, Rinehart & Winston, 1969)

The Psychology of Open Teaching and Learning (Little Brown, 1972)

Real Learning (Little Brown, 1976)

How to Discipline Without Feeling Guilty (Dutton, 1980; Research Press, 1981)

Confident Parenting (Warner, 1988)

When Your Child Is Difficult (Research Press, 1995)

Active Learning (Allyn & Bacon, 1996)

Teaching Actively (Allyn & Bacon, 2006)